T0168792

The Effects of Perstempo on Officer Retention in the U.S. Military

Ronald D. Fricker, Jr.

Prepared for the Office of the Secretary of Defense

National Defense Research Institute

RAND

Approved for public release; distribution unlimited

The research described in this report was sponsored by the Office of the Secretary of Defense (OSD). The research was conducted in RAND's National Defense Research Institute, a federally funded research and development center supported by the OSD, the Joint Staff, the unified commands, and the defense agencies under Contract DASW01-01-C-0004.

Library of Congress Cataloging-in-Publication Data

Fricker, Ronald D., 1960–
    The effects of Perstempo on officer retention in the U.S. military / Ronald D. Fricker.
        p. cm.
    "MR-1556."
    Includes bibliographical references.
    ISBN 0-8330-3176-7
    1. United States—Armed Forces—Officers. 2. United States—Armed Forces—Appointments and retirements. 3. United States—Armed Forces—Personnel management. I. Title.

UB413 .F75 2002
355.1'11'093—dc21

                                                              2002069722

RAND is a nonprofit institution that helps improve policy and decisionmaking through research and analysis. RAND® is a registered trademark. RAND's publications do not necessarily reflect the opinions or policies of its research sponsors.

Published 2002 by RAND
1700 Main Street, P.O. Box 2138, Santa Monica, CA 90407-2138
1200 South Hayes Street, Arlington, VA 22202-5050
201 North Craig Street, Suite 102, Pittsburgh, PA 15213-1516
RAND URL: http://www.rand.org/
To order RAND documents or to obtain additional information, contact Distribution Services: Telephone: (310) 451-7002; Fax: (310) 451-6915; Email: order@rand.org

The operational pace of the United States military has increased dramatically since the end of the Cold War. With an officer corps 31-percent smaller in 2000 compared with 1986, today's military personnel face deployments of increasing frequency, many of which are unplanned and unforeseen.

It is often asserted that this increase in operational tempo has a negative effect on personnel retention. The most commonly cited evidence comes from surveys of servicemembers about their likes and dislikes of military service. Here we evaluate actual behavior, by linking measures of deployment by individual officer to information about if and when each officer leaves the military, to determine whether increased deployments are in fact associated with decreased retention.

The audiences for whom this report is intended include military and civilian officials responsible for doctrine and policy related to the retention and promotion of U.S. military officers, as well as the wider defense policy community concerned with the effects of perstempo on force readiness and personnel retention.

This research was conducted for the Assistant Secretary of Defense (Force Management Policy) within the Forces and Resources Policy Center of RAND's National Defense Research Institute, a federally funded research and development center sponsored by the Office of the Secretary of Defense, the Joint Staff, the unified commands, and the defense agencies.

CONTENTS

FIGURES

TABLES

Since the end of the Gulf War, the operational tempo of the military services has increased dramatically. By some accounts, deployments have increased anywhere from 60 percent (GAO, 1999) to 300 percent (Peters, 1997) between 1986 and 2000 for a force that has 700,000 fewer members and an officer corps that is 31-percent smaller. With recent retention shortfalls, it is often alleged that increased deployments are causing personnel losses. The most commonly cited evidence of this comes from surveys of servicemembers who are queried about their likes and dislikes of military service.[1] While surveys of intentions, and other voiced dissatisfactions with military service, are important tools for identifying areas that require attention, it is just as important to evaluate actual behavior. The relevant question is whether such stated dissatisfaction translates into action so that increased deployments actually result in decreased retention.

Our approach for evaluating whether deployment is associated with changes in retention was to take data on the officer corps for the Army, Navy, Marine Corps, and Air Force; calculate the deployments each officer experienced; and link this information to whether and for how long each officer remained on active duty. We derive the measures of deployment from pay records (Imminent Danger Pay and Family Separation Allowance [FSA]) and each individual's unit association. Given this information, and other such demographic information as occupation, rank, education, gender, and race, we modeled officers at two major phases of their careers: (1) junior offi-

---

[1]See, for example, GAO (1999).

cers immediately after the expiration of the initial service obligation, O-2s and junior O-3s at roughly four to five years of service, and (2) midgrade officers (O-3s and O-4s) with between five and ten years of service.

We employed standard statistical modeling techniques to account for differences in retention patterns by occupation and demographics before looking for a relationship between deployment and retention. We evaluated the effects of two types of deployment, hostile and nonhostile, given that it is reasonable to expect that hostile deployment may affect personnel very differently than nonhostile deployment.

WHAT DID WE LEARN?

Our findings both confirm and contradict some of the common assumptions about the association between deployment and retention of officers. For example, we find a clear *positive* association between increasing amounts of nonhostile deployments and junior and midgrade officer retention: Officers who participate in more nonhostile deployments are *retained* at a higher rate in all services. Hostile deployment generally mitigates this positive effect but, in almost all cases examined, even those with some or all hostile deployment show higher retention rates than nondeployers.

Thus, in contradiction to the common consensus, deployment is *not* associated with higher attrition. However, in the late 1990s, junior officers with higher amounts of hostile deployment are generally associated with lower retention rates compared with junior officers who had the same amount of nonhostile deployment. This effect is most pronounced in the Air Force. For midgrade officers, however, three of the four services show a mitigation or mild reversal of the effect of hostile deployment—meaning that hostile deployment is associated with even higher retention rates—an effect likely attributed to self-selection.

In summary, for the time period we examined (1990–1999) and for the observed levels of deployment, the fundamental trend for junior and midgrade officers was that more deployment was associated with higher retention. For junior officers, hostile deployment tended to lessen, but not eliminate, the positive association with retention.

For midgrade officers, the effects of hostile deployment were even less and may even have had a slightly positive effect for Navy and Marine Corps officers.

HYPOTHESES UNLIKELY TO BE TRUE

While we cannot prove in this study that more deployment caused higher retention, our results cast doubt on other hypotheses.

"More Deployment Causes Lower Retention"

Our results clearly show that more deployment—at least long and/or hostile deployment as we have modeled—was associated with higher retention. If more long and/or hostile deployment caused lower retention, we would expect to observe this in our data. Because we observe the opposite, we can conclude that this hypothesis is not likely to be true, at least in the aggregate for populations similar to those we observed and for episodes of long and/or hostile deployment of the kind experienced in our study period.

This does not mean that, on an individual-by-individual basis, more deployment might cause particular officers to have lower probabilities of remaining in the military. Nor does it mean that increased amounts of deployment, greater than those observed in our data, would not cause a decrease in retention. However, within the constraints of our data we can safely conclude that increased amounts of long and/or hostile deployment did *not* result in lower retention.

"Hostile Deployment Causes Lower Retention"

For Army, Navy, and Marine Corps midgrade officers, using the same logic as in the previous case, we conclude that this hypothesis is probably false. If this hypothesis were true, we would see greater and more-consistent effects than the data show for midgrade officers. For junior officers, on the other hand, this hypothesis may be true in the sense that among those junior officers with the same amount of deployment, we generally observe lower retention among those with a larger fraction of hostile deployment. However, hostile deployment does not result in lower retention rates compared with those who do not deploy.

WHAT THESE DEPLOYMENT MEASURES REPRESENT

Our measures capture only particular types of deployment. Because they were constructed from pay records, our deployments are either long periods away from home and/or excursions into hostile regions of the world. Thus, in addition to capturing long actual deployments (more than 30 days), they also capture long unaccompanied tours of duty in which an individual received FSA. Hence, when we use the term "deployment," we are referring to either periods away from home in which the servicemember (or a sizable fraction of the servicemember's unit) drew FSA, or a period in which the servicemember drew Hostile Fire Pay.

Such a measure of deployment is relevant and important to study. For example, while unaccompanied tours are not "deployments" in the traditional sense, such long periods away from home and family can be hard on servicemembers. This measure represents those excursions away from home that are more likely to

- Individually impose a large burden on the servicemember and his or her family because of their length of time away from home and/or exposure to danger

- Concern operations that are militarily important and that are likely to involve the servicemember in his or her primary military job

- Be predictable, in the case of the nonhostile deployments, when compared with other deployments of shorter duration (less than 30 days).

These last two points may be important distinctions because nonhostile deployments of shorter duration are not captured in these data. We hypothesize that these deployments are typically less predictable and/or more oriented toward routine activities and training. If so, they are of a fundamentally different nature than the deployments we examine here and, given the necessary data, are worthy of a separate analysis as they may have an entirely different effect on servicemembers and their retention decisions.

There are a number of possible explanations for why these results are at such odds with the common wisdom that deployment is bad for retention:

- **Perception versus reality.** It may be that deployment is perceived as negative when, in fact, it has exactly the opposite effect. For example, it could be that servicemembers find deployment a convenient or socially acceptable scapegoat on surveys. However, the evidence, from this work and Hosek and Totten (1998), for long and/or hostile deployments certainly does not support the popular negative perception of deployment.

- **Alternate types of deployment *are* negative.** However, it also may be that the types of deployment captured with our measures have an aggregate positive effect because of their nature, while other types of deployment we could not capture with our pay-based measures are negative. For example, it may be that short, unplanned or unforeseen deployments—not included in our data—have a strongly negative effect.[2]

- **Self-selection mechanisms.** It also could be that those officers with the greatest dislike of deployment self-select into nondeploying positions prior to exiting the military.

- **Aggregation effects.** These results characterize how aggregates of officers responded to particular patterns of hostile and non-hostile deployment. As such, they shed little light on how a particular *individual* officer would respond if he or she experienced one or more additional deployments.

DIRECTIONS FOR FUTURE RESEARCH

There are a number of important directions in which to take this research:

- **Evaluating the effect of short and/or unplanned deployments.** Based on the results of this work, we hypothesize that short and/

---

[2]Some of the services have implemented efforts to make deployment more predictable, such as the Air Force reconfiguration into expeditionary forces. If the hypothesis is that unplanned and unforeseen deployment has the greatest negative effect, then efforts to improve deployment predictability should be very beneficial.

or unplanned deployments may have a negative impact on retention. The new data currently being collected by the services will contain information about short deployments and will permit evaluation of this hypothesis once sufficient data are collected.

- **Accounting for officer quality.** This work has found that increasing amounts of deployment are associated with higher retention rates, yet it is not known how deployment affects the overall quality of the officer corps. This is an important issue because the observed aggregate effects could be masking important differential effects. For example, lower-quality officers may have fewer civilian opportunities so that they may be more likely to endure a level of deployment that would cause higher-quality officers to leave.

- **Detailed modeling of specific communities.** Detailed modeling would allow us to account for differences within each community and to better investigate the causal question. For example, hostile deployment appears to have negative effects for Navy junior officers in legal occupations. This is different from all of the other Navy occupational categories.

- **Evaluating the extent of self-selection.** To put these results in a better context, it is necessary to improve our understanding of how much influence officers have on their future job assignments, particularly how that selection impacts their likelihood of deployment *and* their likelihood of remaining on active duty.

ACKNOWLEDGMENTS

I am particularly indebted to James Hosek and Mark Totten, RAND colleagues, who were instrumental in laying the foundation for this research. Not only does this work build upon their prior research evaluating the effects of perstempo on enlisted reenlistment, but Jim provided invaluable guidance and assistance during the course of the research and the modeling could not have been completed without Mark's masterful programming.

This research was sponsored by Curtis Gilroy in the Office of the Under Secretary of Defense for Personnel and Readiness and it has greatly benefited from his interest and support. This work also benefited from the perstempo conference sponsored by David S.C. Chu, Under Secretary of Defense for Personnel and Readiness, in October 2001. The interaction with Dr. Chu, his staff, and the researchers brought together in the conference helped crystallize some of these ideas.

I am also indebted to Michael Dove, Hannah Shin, Angella McGinnis, and Eugene Lee of the Defense Manpower Data Center for compiling the original Perstempo database and for providing subsequent updates without which this effort would have been impossible.

The clarity and accuracy of the manuscript has been significantly improved as a result of Richard Buddin's and Beth Asch's thoughtful and insightful reviews of early drafts. Any errors or omissions are solely my responsibility.

ABBREVIATIONS

BRAC	Base Realignment and Closure
DMDC	Defense Manpower Data Center
DoD	Department of Defense
FSA	Family Separation Allowance
GAO	U.S. General Accounting Office
HFP	Hostile Fire Pay
HR	Hazard ratio
ISC	Inter-Service Separation Code
IT/MIS	Information technology/ management information sciences
OR	Odds ratio
OUSD(P&R)	Office of the Under Secretary of Defense for Personnel and Readiness
Perstempo	Personnel tempo
UIC	Unit identification code

Chapter One

INTRODUCTION

The operational pace or tempo (optempo) of the United States military has increased dramatically since the end of the Cold War. Today's military personnel face deployments of increasing frequency, many of which are unplanned and unforeseen. By some accounts, deployments have increased by anywhere from 60 percent (GAO, 1999) to 300 percent (Peters, 1997) between 1986 and 2000, with an officer corps that is 31-percent smaller (Table 1.1).[1] In the Air Force, for example, 15,000 airmen are now deployed at any given time, compared with only about 2,000 before the Gulf War. While the Marines were involved in 15 contingency operations between 1982 and 1989, they have participated in more than 62 of these operations since 1989 (Peters, 1997).

There is reason to believe that increases in deployment may have a negative impact on retention. For example, in the 1999 Survey of Active Duty Personnel, servicemembers were asked, "Even if you have no plans to leave, . . . which is the most important factor for leaving or considering leaving active duty?" Of 37 possible responses, across all ranks and paygrades (both officer and enlisted), deployment was ranked as the fifth-highest reason and, similarly,

---

[1] Differences in the reported rates of deployment differ for many reasons, including methods of accounting and even the definition of "deployment." In fact, as we will discuss, defining and subsequently measuring "deployment" is difficult. For example, some deployment measures count any time away from home, even when the servicemember is only away on a temporary duty assignment, say for training, while others do not. However, most deployment measures do agree on one thing: The overall rate of "deployment" is up.

Table 1.1

Number of Active-Duty Commissioned Officers by Service

	Fiscal Year		% Change
	1986[a]	2000[b]	
Army	94,845	65,353	−31
Navy	68,922	51,540	−25
Marine Corps	18,734	16,017	−15
Air Force	109,051	69,022	−37
Total DoD	291,552	201,932	−31

[a]OUSD(P&R), 1999, Table D-25.
[b]Gordon, Gelfeld, and Smith (2001).
NOTE: Not including warrant officers.

when asked the second most important reason, deployment was ranked seventh-highest out of 37 (Table 1.2).

Junior officers (O-1s to O-3s) were even slightly more likely to indicate that deployment was either the most important or second most important reason, both in terms of percentage indicating that deployment was the most important or second most important factor, and in terms of a slight increase in the relative ranking of

Table 1.2

Top Seven Most Important and Second Most Important Reasons for Leaving Active Duty (All Services, Ranks, and Paygrades Combined)

	Most Important Reason		Second Most Important Reason	
	Percentage	Rank	Percentage	Rank
Basic pay	28.1	1	10.9	1
Amount of personal family time	8.8	2	7.2	2
Quality of leadership	8.2	3	6.7	3
Amount of enjoyment from job	6.9	4	5.8	6
Deployment	6.1	5	4.8	7
Retirement pay	5.0	6	6.6	4
Pace of promotions	4.9	7	5.9	5

SOURCE: Tabulations of responses from DMDC (2000).

deployment among the other possible factors (Table 1.3).[2] Similarly, in a General Accounting Office (GAO) survey of active duty officers in "retention critical" specialties, frequency of deployments was listed in the top five reasons to leave the military. The GAO (1999) said

> many factors were sources of dissatisfaction and reasons to leave the military. The majority of factors (62 percent) were associated with work circumstances such as the lack of equipment and materials to successfully complete the demands of daily job requirements, the undermanning of units, the frequency of deployments, and the lack of personal time for family.

The commonly accepted wisdom is that such negative opinions of deployment have a direct effect on retention. Simply stated, it is generally believed that the increased pace of deployment in the military is causing servicemembers to leave active duty. But does opinion actually translate into action? While surveys such as the Survey of Active Duty Personnel provide valuable feedback to military decisionmakers, it is just as important to evaluate actual behavior to see whether increasing rates of deployment are in fact associated with decreased retention.

Table 1.3

Top Six Most Important and Second Most Important Reasons for Leaving Active Duty (O-1 to O-3 Officers, All Services)

	Most Important Reason		Second Most Important Reason	
	Percentage	Rank	Percentage	Rank
Basic pay	15.5	1	9.9	1
Amount of personal family time	13.6	2	9.8	2
Amount of enjoyment from job	12.4	3	7.2	3
Deployment	8.3	4	6.1	6
Quality of leadership	7.9	5	7.0	4
Retirement pay	4.8	6	6.3	5

SOURCE: Tabulations of responses from DMDC (2000).

---

[2]"Pace of promotions" dropped significantly in the rankings by junior officers and therefore is not included in the officer tabulations.

Hosek and Totten (1998) conducted such an evaluation, studying the effect of deployments, both long and hostile, on the retention rates for enlisted personnel. They found that, among personnel who had no long or hostile duty, some deployment experience actually *increases* the likelihood of reenlistment. However, for those personnel who have already had some long or hostile duty, additional deployment tends to reduce the likelihood of reenlistment. They concluded that "while long or hostile duty is a 'good thing,' there can be too much of a good thing, particularly if it involves danger" (Hosek and Totten, 1998, p. xi). An equivalent analysis has not been conducted for military officers.

In this report, we investigate the association between long and/or hostile deployment duty and the retention of junior and midgrade officers. Unlike enlisted personnel, officers do not join the military for a fixed period.[3] They also tend to have more control than do enlisted personnel over future assignments, which implies that they may have some influence on their chance of deploying.[4] Also, officers are more likely to be career oriented, older, and thus more mature than junior-enlisted personnel. For these and other reasons, it is not appropriate to assume Hosek and Totten's enlisted results apply to officers.

Because of differences in titles, we refer to the various officer ranks by their alphanumeric designation (O-1, O-2, etc.). Most officers enter active duty as O-1s—ensigns in the Navy and second lieutenants in the other services. It takes approximately two years for promotion to O-2 and another two years to O-3. Promotion through these junior officer ranks to O-3 is quite predictable and virtually all

---

[3]As we will discuss in the next chapter, officers often begin their military careers with a "service obligation," which is a period of time they are required to remain on active duty, generally in return for some kind of financial support for education. However, officers do not sign contracts to serve for fixed periods of time like enlisted personnel do.

[4]In general, officers have at least some input into the process of selecting their future duty assignments via an officer "detailing" system (or variants thereof), though the extent of the input varies by service, occupation, and rank. Hence, officers often have the option to choose among a number of future assignments, some of which may be known to deploy more or less than others. Because of this, we cannot make the analytically simplifying assumption that deployment is exogenous (i.e., external) to the officer.

officers make these promotions. Time in grade for O-3s and O-4s is approximately five years. Promotion in these midgrade officer ranks is less certain, and the time to promotion is more variable.

Under this promotion schedule, officers generally reach the rank of O-4 with between eight and ten years of service. Officers can retire after 20 years of service, though promotion to O-5 is required to accrue the requisite number of years.[5]

Unlike enlisted servicemembers, officers may choose to leave the military at any time, though this decision may be subject to some constraints. These constraints often involve "service obligations"—a requirement to remain on active duty for some length of time. Service obligations are usually incurred in return for some type of education or training. In fact, most officers assume an initial service obligation when some or all of their college education is funded by the military, perhaps at a service academy or at a university with a Reserve Officer Training Corps (ROTC) program.[6] For example, newly commissioned officers from the military academies incur five-year active-duty service obligations.[7] After the initial service obligation, officers may incur other service obligations for advanced training or education. The extent and duration of these obligations vary by service.

---

[5]If the officer had prior enlisted service time, or other federal government or military service time, then that could count toward retirement. However, as we will later discuss, we will only model the effects of deployment on officers without prior service.

[6]Some officers may enter the service without a service obligation, generally because they did not rely on the military to fund their college education. However, the majority of officers do incur a service obligation.

[7]In addition to an active-duty service obligation, some officers may also incur an additional obligation in the reserves. In this report, because we are concerned only with active-duty retention, when we refer to "service obligation," we specifically mean active-duty service obligation.

Chapter Two

DEPLOYMENT RATES AND MEASURES

POSSIBLE EFFECTS OF DEPLOYMENT

Anecdotally, the effects of deployment can be hypothesized to be both desirable and undesirable; they can also be construed to help or hinder careers. For example, we have heard secondhand accounts of officers being reassigned to a deploying unit in place of a necessary career-advancing tour. As a result, these officers may be unable to get a requisite "ticket punched" (that is, get a required type of job to prepare for advancement) and then may subsequently be passed over for promotion. If such occurrences are common, then deployments will clearly interfere with retention, both directly and indirectly through decreases in officer corps morale. Conversely, we have also heard some officers say that the right type of successful deployment can enhance an individual's chances for promotion, as it distinguishes that individual from his or her contemporaries in a relevant manner.

It has also been related to us that many servicemembers find deployment enjoyable because it allows them to exercise their primary military skills and deployment can result in additional financial compensation.[1] Furthermore, deployments often take the service-

---

[1] Personnel separated from their families for more than 30 days receive a Family Separation Allowance (FSA). It is paid to military personnel stationed abroad on unaccompanied tours, afloat, or deployed in military operations. There are two types of FSAs, and the amount of compensation changes over time. Personnel who deploy to areas deemed "hostile" can additionally receive Hostile Fire Pay (HFP). (HFP is now called Imminent Danger Pay. Because our data cover the earlier period when it was called

member out of the day-to-day peacetime routine, which tends to involve inspections and other more-mundane aspects of military life, and involves them in the operational aspects of their career. Without exception, all military officers we have talked to enjoy this aspect of deploying. On the other hand, deployments bring separation from family and other hardships, and the determination of whether the positives outweigh these negatives is very much an individual decision.

The type and quantity of deployment, as well as each individual's taste and expectations for deployment, have a direct impact on whether or not one enjoys the deployment experience and, if not, whether the negative experience is enough to cause the individual to leave the military. For example, participation in the Gulf War is generally cited by many servicemembers as a positive experience that outweighed their personal sacrifice to home and family life. Frequent peacekeeping missions may not carry the same operational importance and warfighting immediacy, and thus may not balance out the negative aspects of deployment as well.

Taste and expectation also play a large role in satisfaction with deployments. For example, over the years, we have found that members of forces with operational missions that require frequent deployments tend to be very satisfied with their experiences. However, it is not clear whether this satisfaction results because these individuals self-select into such careers or whether the experiences of operational deployments are positive, or some combination of the two.

In summary, the effect of deployment on an officer's decision to stay in the military is not obvious and is probably very complex. In this work, because of the limitations in our data and in retrospective studies, we cannot explore the causal relationship between deployment and retention.[2] We do, however, evaluate whether there is an

---

HFP, and to be consistent with Hosek and Totten, we will continue to refer to it as HFP.) Personnel can also receive tax advantages and deferments during deployment.

[2]Ideally, to evaluate the question of the causality between perstempo and retention, deployments would have to be randomly assigned to officers. However, as we have previously discussed, officers can influence their assignments, and thus their likelihood of deployment, so assuming that deployments are randomly assigned to officers is not valid. Matching officers into "closely similar" cohorts, based on tastes for the

association between deployment and officer retention. This is an important distinction. A determination of association simply means we find that, for example, as one factor increases, then so does the other. This does not, however, necessarily imply that the first factor causes the second.

OUR MEASURES OF DEPLOYMENT

The measures of deployment we use are the same as those originally created and used by Hosek and Totten (1998). They are based on the receipt of special pays military personnel receive when deployments separate them from their families or they are deployed to a hostile area. The two pays are FSA and HFP, respectively.[3]

We use the Hosek and Totten measures for a number of reasons. First, we are interested in directly comparing our results for officers with those Hosek and Totten found for enlisted personnel. Keeping the deployment measures consistent makes the comparison easier and clearer. Second, alternate measures of deployment are not yet readily available. Hosek and Totten provide a detailed description and justification for these deployment measures. Here we provide only a brief summary.

Episodes of Long or Hostile Deployment

This measure counts the number of deployments in a 36-month period.[4] An episode begins when an individual's record shows evi-

---

military and deployment, conditions for deployment, career intentions, etc., would allow us to take a step closer in investigating causal relationships, but such data are not available.

[3]While we previously noted that deployment can result in financial advantages to the servicemember, HFP and FSA (Type II) are not likely to influence an officer to seek deployment. For example, an O-3 with five years of service and dependents would have had a gross monthly salary of approximately $3,700, not including any special pays (Basic Pay: $2,926.80; Basic Allowance for Quarters with dependents: $614.40; Basic Allowance for Subsistence: $149.67. Source: Office of the Secretary of Defense, 1996). In comparison, HFP was $150 per month and FSA (Type II) was $75 per month. Hence, at most, these deployment-related pays represented a 6-percent increase in gross compensation.

[4]Totten and Hosek used the 24-month period prior to six months before the service-member's decision to reenlist or leave.

dence of deployment either via receipt of FSA or HFP, or via a Defense Manpower Data Center (DMDC)–derived deployment indicator[5] for a particular month. The episode continues for as long as the individual's record shows evidence of deployment. Thus, we start by observing the receipt of FSA, HFP, or a DMDC deployment indicator, and we count as one episode the entire period of time until we observe a month when neither FSA nor HFP was received, and the DMDC deployment indicator is off.

Note that to collect FSA, a deployment must be more than 30 days. Therefore, the FSA portion of the measure misses deployments of less than 30 days. Furthermore, because the perstempo data is aggregated to the monthly level, the use of HFP may also undercount the number of episodes when an individual is involved in many short hostile deployments. This can occur in two ways: (1) if an individual makes two or more deployments in one month, the data will only show the receipt of HFP for that month, which we can only interpret as one deployment; and, (2) if the individual makes two or more short deployments in separate, adjacent months, the two months will be counted as one deployment.

The episode measure (of long or hostile deployment) is used to capture the effect of the number of deployments to which individuals are exposed. The hypothesis is that each deployment represents a separate disruption of the individual's home and work life, just as each deployment offers a fresh opportunity to employ skills and training in a military activity or operation. The cumulative effect of multiple deployments may have a negative or positive effect on retention.

---

[5]As discussed in Hosek and Totten (1998), single personnel are not eligible for FSA so that, in the absence of any other measure, deployments for personnel without dependents would be undercounted. DMDC has derived another deployment measure based at the unit level. This measure uses information from unit personnel with dependents to decide if the unit was deployed. If so, then all personnel in the unit are given a deployed indicator. In essence, this measure uses FSA plus HFP for personnel with dependents to impute deployment for those without dependents.

Months of Long or Hostile Deployment

In contrast to episodes, this measure captures the effect of the duration of deployment. As with episodes, deployment in a particular
month is determined by the receipt of HFP or FSA, or by the DMDC
deployment indicator. However, this measure simply adds the total
number of months an individual was deployed in a three-year
period. As such, this measure captures the effect of length of
deployment with the idea that the cumulative amount of time individuals are deployed might have a positive, negative, or perhaps
reversing (e.g., quadratic) relationship with retention.

WHAT THESE "DEPLOYMENT" MEASURES REPRESENT

Our measures capture only particular types of "deployment."
Because of the way they were constructed from pay records, these
deployments are either long periods away from home and/or excursions into hostile regions. Thus, in addition to capturing long actual
deployments (more than 30 days), they also capture long unaccompanied tours of duty in which an individual received FSA. Hence,
when we use the term "deployment" in this work, we are referring to
either periods away from home in which the servicemember (or a
sizable fraction of the servicemember's unit) drew FSA, or a period in
which the servicemember drew HFP.

Such a measure of deployment is relevant and important to study.
For example, while unaccompanied tours are not "deployments" in
the traditional sense, such long periods away from home and family
can be hard on servicemembers. What this measure represents are
those excursions that are more likely to

• Impose a large burden on the servicemember and his or her
  family because of their length of time away from home and/or
  exposure to danger,

• Represent, in the case of hostile deployments, deployments that
  are militarily important and likely to involve the servicemember
  in his or her primary military job, and/or

• Be predictable, in the case of the nonhostile deployments, when
  compared with other deployments of shorter duration (less than
  30 days).

These last two points may be important distinctions because non-hostile deployments of shorter duration are not captured in these data. We hypothesize that these deployments are, generally, of a less predictable nature and/or more oriented toward routine activities. If so, they are of a fundamentally different nature than the deployments we examine here and, given the necessary data, are worthy of a separate analysis as they may have an entirely different effect on servicemembers and their retention decisions.

GENERAL TRENDS DURING THE PERIOD OF INTEREST

We divide the 1990s into two distinct periods, the "early 1990s" (1995 and pre-1995) and the "late 1990s" (post-1995). The early 1990s correspond to a period of contraction in the U.S. military, characterized by a significant downsizing of the force and a very public and contentious process of closing military bases and facilities that culminated in three rounds of Base Realignment and Closures (Figure 2.1). In contrast, the late 1990s was a period of relative stability with most of the downsizing completed, or least determined and, from that point on, reasonably predictable.

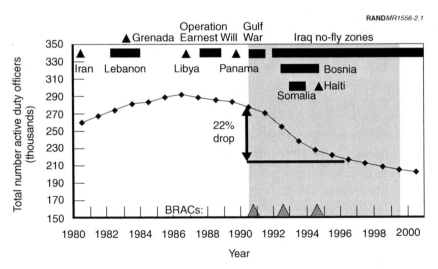

Figure 2.1—Historical Officer Corps Size and Major Events, 1980–2000

Deployment trends were something of the opposite, with an increasing fraction of each service's personnel deployed as the decade progressed (Figures 2.2–2.5), particularly as compared with the late 1980s. Of course, each service experienced a significant spike in deployments in 1991, corresponding to the Gulf War, but a clear increasing trend in the general pace of deployments continued thereafter.

Figures 2.2–2.5 show the pace of deployments for the Army, Navy, Marine Corps, and Air Force quarterly from December 1987 to December 1992 and monthly thereafter through March 1998. The

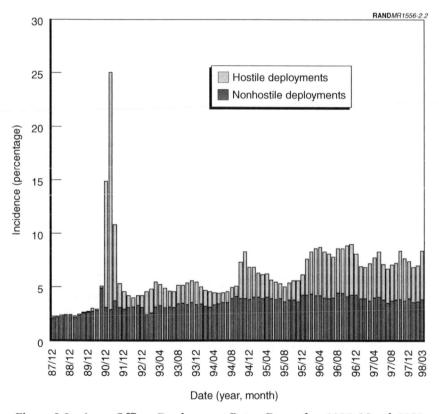

Figure 2.2—Army Officer Deployment Rates, December 1987–March 1998

vertical axis is the percentage of the service's officer corps deployed during that period (month or quarter).

The Army (Figure 2.1) and the Air Force (Figure 2.4) show the most significant increases in deployment rates when compared with their pre–Gulf War deployment rates. For example, deployments to Bosnia in late 1994 and 1995 are clearly visible in the figures. The Navy and Marine Corps also show increases, though more modest. On the other hand, their pre–Gulf War deployment rates were already significantly higher than the other two services.

The figures also appear to show the deployment rates of all the services roughly stabilizing sometime in post-1995. That is, after 1995,

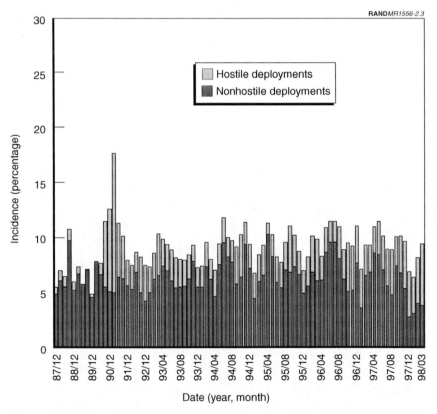

Figure 2.3—Navy Officer Deployment Rates, December 1987–March 1998

for the Army and Air Force, the rate of deployment looks relatively constant, generally above the early 1990s deployment rates, and at a pace significantly higher than that of the late 1980s. The Marine Corps actually seems to show a slight decrease in the late 1990s, while the Navy deployment rate is essentially unchanged (with the exception of the spike for the Gulf War).

Connecting these trends to officer retention, at least in terms of comparing one trend with the other, is slightly more difficult. One reason is that officer retention in the early 1990s was artificially high because of the stop-loss instituted during the Gulf War. As shown in Figure 2.6, none of the services experienced any meaningful loss of

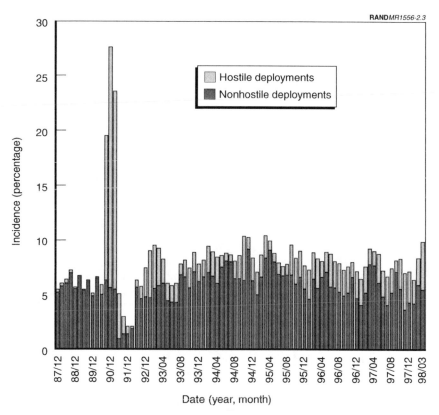

Figure 2.4—Marine Corps Officer Deployment Rates,
December 1987–March 1998

personnel during the Gulf War period as a result of stop-loss. After that, however, retention decreased during the early 1990s—from its artificial high in the Gulf War—again to stabilize for each service in the mid-1990s.

The percentages in Figure 2.6 are for the fraction of O-3s who were still on active duty one year after the expiration of their initial service obligation. The interservice trends shown in Figure 2.6 are well known. The Marine Corps tends to have the highest retention rate, followed by the Air Force. The Army and Navy rates are lower, with the Army showing better retention than the Navy in the early 1990s and the reverse in the late 1990s.

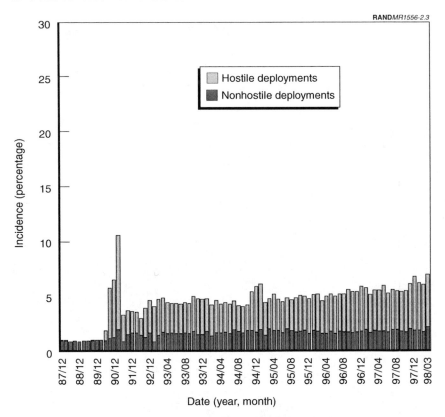

Figure 2.5—Air Force Officer Deployment Rates,
December 1987–March 1998

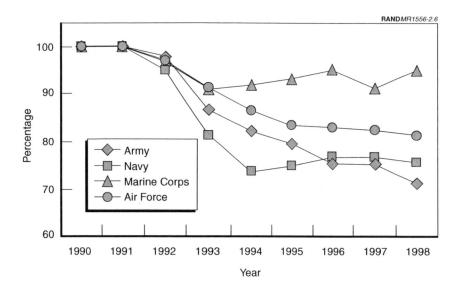

Figure 2.6—Trends in the Percentage of O-3s Retained One Year After Expiration of Minimum Service Obligation

Chapter Three

ANALYTIC APPROACH AND DATA

It is difficult to take raw trends in deployment and retention, such as those shown in the previous chapter, and draw meaningful conclusions from them for a number of reasons. The most important reason is that there are many factors that affect retention besides deployment and, prior to drawing any conclusion about the relationship between deployment and retention, it is vitally important to account for those other factors. For example, there are known differences in retention by occupation, gender, and whether a servicemember has dependents. The methods we employ allow such factors to be accounted for prior to evaluating how deployment is related to retention.

Our data were drawn from the Perstempo database provided by DMDC. The initial database consisted of all officers on active duty between December 1987 and March 1998. This was subsequently updated with data through September 1999. The resulting combined database gives quarterly "snapshots" for the first five years (December 1987–December 1992) and monthly thereafter. For junior officers, we subset the data to those officers commissioned after December 1986, whose initial service obligation ended before September 1998, and whom we could identify as not having been involuntarily separated from military service.[1] For midgrade officers,

---

[1] To determine personnel who were not involuntarily separated, we obtained the Inter-Service Separation Code (ISC) from DMDC for each individual and removed from our database those with an ISC greater than 05. These are personnel who were separated for the following reasons: medical disqualifications, dependency or hardship, retirement, failure to meet minimum behavioral or performance criteria, etc.

we included those officers whose initial obligation expired between November 1992 and September 1998.

To account for differences in the services' policies, practices, and organizational cultures, we model each service individually, and we further model junior and midgrade officers separately. In particular, we first evaluate junior officer retention at the end of the initial service obligation period. Officers at this stage are primarily O-2s and junior O-3s after about four or five years of service. We then evaluate midcareer officers, O-3s and O-4s, who remained in the service after their initial service obligation.

We model the junior officers separately from the midgrade officers for a number of reasons. First, the initial service obligation provides a definitive point at which to evaluate junior officer retention. This is convenient for modeling and substantively important, as the initial service obligation is incurred before the junior officers have actually been able to experience the military. As a result, they are not fully informed about the consequences of their decision to incur a service obligation, and many will choose to leave the military after this initial obligation. Thus, those officers who remain on active duty after their initial obligation constitute a significantly different group who have made a more informed choice to remain on active duty.

Second, officers who have chosen to remain on active duty after their initial service obligation are then continuously at risk to leave the service at any time. While new service obligations can be incurred, these subsequent service obligations are incurred after the officer has experienced the realities of his or her chosen career, so that these service obligation decisions can be interpreted as confirmation of a career choice. From a modeling standpoint, we assume that an officer who has incurred such an additional obligation has simply made an early decision to remain on active duty for the duration of the obligation.

Note that the ISC was not available for all personnel who had left the service and the percentage varied by service. The assumption we are forced to make is within service, for those personnel who separated in our time period of interest, the ISC is missing randomly.

JUNIOR OFFICER MODELS

We model the effect of deployment on junior officers by looking one year after the expiration of each officer's initial service obligation and evaluating those who remained on active duty versus those who did not. As we discuss in the next subsection, we employed standard statistical modeling techniques (logistic regression) to construct our models. Details about the statistical methodology can be found in Appendix A. For each junior officer, we calculate the number of episodes of long deployment and the number of episodes of hostile deployment for the 36 months prior to the expiration of each officer's initial service obligation. We assigned officers to occupational groupings to capture the effects of occupation (see Appendix D for occupational category definitions). We also incorporate demographic covariates in our models, including gender, race, whether the officer has dependents or not, and accession source (academy graduate or not), to capture the effects of these characteristics on the decision to remain in the military, prior to evaluating the effect of deployment.[2]

Figure 3.1 shows how the deployment measures and the determination of whether an officer has been retained are tied to the date when

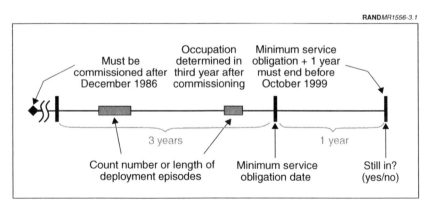

RAND*MR1556-3.1*

Figure 3.1—Definition of the Periods for Allowable Data and When the
Measures Were Constructed for Junior Officer Models

---

[2]Covariates that could vary over time, such as whether an officer has dependents or not, were set based on the officer's status during the quarter of his or her minimum service obligation date.

an officer's minimum service obligation ends. All the characteristics in the model are measured at or before the minimum service obligation date. For example, the deployment measures are calculated for the three years preceding the minimum service obligation date; occupation is determined from the latest occupational data in the third year after commissioning.

Determining Whether a Junior Officer Was Retained

We look one year after expiration of the minimum service obligation. If an officer is still recorded in the Perstempo data file as being on active duty, we make the determination that the officer chose to remain on active duty. If not, we conclude that he or she chose to leave.

Depending on timing and service considerations, an officer may not leave exactly at the expiration of his or her minimum obligated service. The one-year period allows for delays in actually leaving the service. Unlike enlisted personnel, officers do not serve for a fixed period of time and they are formally required to resign their commission to leave the military. This must normally be done with some prior notice, perhaps up to a year in advance. The assumption we make by using the year window is that an officer who leaves within that time period intended to leave the service at the expiration of his or her initial service obligation but may not have been able to actually leave until some time after. Shortening the window could affect the results by classifying some officers as having been retained when, in fact, circumstances required them to stay on active duty for slightly longer than their obligation.

Lengthening the window would likely have less of an effect because those who left within the one-year window would still be classified the same way. However, it could result in classifying a few more individuals as leaving immediately after their obligation date, when instead they had chosen to leave at a later date. The primary effects on the model would be:

• For some individuals, the time between the three years when we measure deployment and when they actually leave would be larger. This might serve to decrease the effect we are trying to measure.

- It would decrease the number of records available for us to build models given that each individual in the data would need to have more than four years of data between December 1986 and September 1999. We thus settled on a one-year window as a reasonable compromise between these two competing requirements.[3]

Definition of Occupational Categories

Service obligations, as well as retention decisions, on average, vary by occupation. For example, pilots and other occupations that are given special training often incur greater initial service obligation periods. Similarly, various occupational skills are in greater or lesser demand in the civilian sector, and some occupations are given incentive pays to increase retention. These factors and others serve to influence retention by occupational category.

In order to account for such effects in our models, we assigned officers to occupational specialty groupings. As shown in Figure 3.1, a junior officer's occupational specialty was determined three years after commissioning, based on the occupational specialty code recorded in the Perstempo database. We allowed the three-year delay so that officers given training and student occupational codes early in their careers had time to have their true occupational codes assigned. For midgrade officers, we used the latest occupational code listed in the data.

We then used the occupational codes[4] to assign officers to one of fifteen categories that we attempted to standardize as much as possible across the services. The occupational categories (see Appendix D for a mapping of occupational codes to occupational categories) are

- acquisition,

---

[3]As part of a sensitivity analysis, we constructed and evaluated models with two-year windows. The results, as expected, were consistent with the one-year window models and were what we expected. The two-year window was to mitigate the observed effect of the deployment effects.

[4]For the Army we used Area of Concentration codes; for the Navy, a combination of Designator codes and Navy Officer Billet Classification codes; for the Marine Corps, Military Occupational Specialty codes; and for the Air Force, Air Force Specialty codes.

- pilot,

- intelligence,

- information technology/management information sciences (IT/MIS),

- legal,

- line,

- medical,

- nuclear power,

- other aviation,

- other/unknown,

- personnel/administration,

- religious,

- scientific/engineering,

- student, and

- supply.

Of these, nuclear power is an occupation unique to the Navy; the Marine Corps does not have codes for medical or religious occupations; the Navy does not have occupational codes for students; and the Air Force has pilots rather than line officers.

Calculation of Initial Service Obligation

Service obligation was available for some officers on the DMDC Master/Loss file. We were interested in modeling whether deployment affected an officer's decision to remain in the service after his or her *initial* service obligation expired. We assumed that if an officer incurred an additional service obligation, then he or she was making the decision to remain in the military—at least beyond his or her initial obligation.

We imputed an initial service obligation for those officers who did not have one in the Master/Loss file. To do this, we first extracted the records from the Master/Loss file that had a service obligation and used the most recent observation between the second and third year after commissioning. We next computed the median service obligation by occupational category and rounded it to the nearest half year. Then, for those records missing service obligation, we assigned them the value for their occupational category; for those with a service obligation, we used the minimum of the actual value or the occupational group median plus two years. That is, we truncated unusually long service obligations to correct for errors and other data anomalies.[5]

Model Covariates

In addition to occupation, we incorporated data on each officer's gender, race, accession source (academy or not), and family status (single or has dependents at the time of expiration of minimum service obligation). These covariates all may have some effect on an individual's decision to remain in the military. We also included indicator covariates for the year each junior officer was eligible to separate from the service (i.e., the year the initial service obligation expired). These "fixed effect" covariates account for year-to-year variation, such as changes in the civilian unemployment rate and temporal changes in each service.

MIDGRADE OFFICER MODELS

Because midgrade officers may leave the service at any time, we model the effect of deployment on midgrade officers differently from

---

[5]The percentage of truncation varied by service. This variation is a function of both service anomalies, such as data quality and recordkeeping practices, and the fraction of service obligations actually recorded in the data. For example, Marine Corps service obligations were entirely imputed because none were available in the data. The result is that none of these imputed service obligations had to be truncated. For the other services, almost 7 percent of the Army, slightly more than 4 percent of the Navy, and almost 19 percent of the Air Force service obligations were truncated.

There are a number of possible explanations for the higher truncation percentage in the Air Force, including differences or errors in recordkeeping and the possibility of a very bimodal distribution for Air Force service obligation times. If, in fact, the truncated service obligation times were correct, then truncation would tend to attenuate the relationship between deployment and retention, as those who were truncated would be counted as choosing to remain on active duty when, in fact, they simply were not able to leave because of their service commitment.

the way we model it on junior officers. We employed another standard statistical modeling technique—survival analysis—to construct our models. Survival analysis models the time to an event where, in this case, we model the time until separation from the service. See Appendix A for details.

An advantage of survival analysis is that it can handle "censored" observations, such as with Officer #1 in Figure 3.2. In this particular case, the Perstempo data ends in September 1999 but Officer #1 is still on active duty. Hence, we know when Officer #1 was commissioned, and all information about this servicemember through September 1999, but we do not know if or when he or she left the service. Survival analysis also handles completely observed cases, such as Officer #2 in Figure 3.2.

As shown in Figure 3.2, for each midgrade officer who remained on active duty after his or her initial service obligation,[6] we calculate the

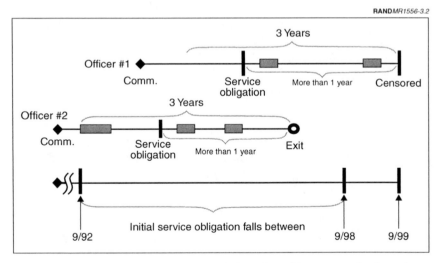

Figure 3.2—Definition of the Periods for Allowable Data and When the Measures Were Constructed for Midgrade Officer Models

[6]Remaining on active duty after the initial service obligation was defined for the midgrade officers exactly as it was for the junior officers. If a midgrade officer was still on active duty one year after his or her initial service obligation period expired, that individual was included in the midgrade officer analysis.

number of long deployments and the number of hostile deployments for the 36 months preceding either the servicemember's exit date or September 1999 if the officer is still on active duty at that point. We use this information, along with covariates similar to those used in the junior officer models (e.g., occupational category, gender, race, whether the officer has dependents or not), to capture the effect of these characteristics on the decision to remain in the military. The models use this quarterly information, along with the information about how long each officer remained on active duty, to determine the effects of deployment on retention.[7]

Definition of Occupational Categories

As with the junior officer models, we assigned midgrade officers to occupational specialty groupings. However, unlike the junior officers, we used the latest occupational code listed in the data. This corresponded either to the occupational code the officer held upon separation from the service or the one held on September 1999, the end of our data. We used the same 15 categories listed above, which were standardized as much as possible across the services.

Model Covariates

In addition to the covariates from the junior officer models (gender, race, accession source, family status), we incorporated time-varying covariates for rank, educational level, whether the officer had been promoted in the last year, whether the officer had received an advanced degree in the past two years, and indicators for each year. The year indicators have the same role in these models as they do in the junior officer models: to account for year-to-year variation that affects the decision to separate from the service.

---

[7]Survival models can easily incorporate "time-varying" covariates, such as dependent status. This allows the model to explicitly account for demographic characteristics that can change with time. For our models, the time-varying covariates are rank, whether an officer had dependents, educational status, whether the officer was promoted in the last year, and whether the officer obtained an advanced degree in the last two years.

The promotion and advanced degree receipt indicators were included since these affect the individual's inclination or ability to separate. In the case of degree receipt (from an educational program funded by the Department of Defense [DoD]), officers in all services incur a service obligation, so an individual has a much lower likelihood of separation after receiving a degree. For the promotion indicators, some services require the promoted officer to attend a service school, after which the officer incurs an additional service obligation. For those who do not, it is also reasonable to assume that promotion is likely to positively influence, and reflect, the decision to remain on active duty.

Chapter Four

THE EFFECTS OF PERSTEMPO ON RETENTION

In this chapter, we first present our findings for each service, synthesizing the results for both junior and midgrade officers. We then discuss the results in general for junior officers, followed by those for midgrade officers. We do not dwell on specific numerical values but emphasize overall trends. We also tend not to describe our results in terms of statistical significance as the data comprise the entire population.[1]

We present the results for junior officers in terms of *odds ratios* (*OR*), which are ratios of the odds of separation for a given deployment pattern (e.g., two deployments: one hostile and one nonhostile) versus the odds of separation for those with no deployment. As discussed in Appendix A, the odds ratio can be roughly interpreted as a relative risk. This means, for example, that if the *OR* = 2 then officers with the characteristic are roughly twice as likely to leave active duty as those without.

Midgrade officer results are presented in terms of *hazard ratios* (*HR*). The hazard ratio is interpreted as a comparison of the probability of separation for an officer with a certain level and type of deployment with a similar individual without any deployment. If the ratio is larger than one, there is a higher risk of separation for those who deploy than for those who do not; if it is less than one, the risk is less

---

[1]Standard statistical methodology presumes that the data are a sample from a larger population. Given such a sample, most statistical tests then proceed to evaluate whether a particular property of the statistic can be determined after accounting for sampling error. For this data, there is no sampling error.

for those who deploy. (See Appendix A for theoretical details and Appendix B for complete model specification and results.)

For both junior and midgrade officers, our model specification allowed evaluation of whether there were differences in deployment patterns in the early and late 1990s. As we discussed in the previous chapter, there are a number of reasons to expect differences in the two periods, including significant external events that could have affected attitudes about military life in general and deployment in particular and/or the changing nature of the deployments themselves. Certainly deployment in the early 1990s with Operations Desert Shield and Desert Storm was a unique experience. We will discuss the observed differences more fully with the results for each individual service.

RESULTS BY SERVICE

Figures 4.1–4.4 summarize the results of our findings by service. These figures combine four separate sets of results for both junior officers and midgrade officers for the early and late 1990s. The quad layout allows comparison of temporal trends within a particular grade group (junior or midgrade officers) and comparisons between the grade groups for a particular time period. Each plot has the total number of deployment episodes on the horizontal axis and either the odds ratio or the hazard ratio of separation on the vertical axis. Within a particular number of deployments the bars represent the number of hostile deployments, starting from the black bars for "no hostile deployments" out of the total and proceeding through the white bars that indicate that all of the deployments were hostile.

Each bar represents a comparison of the odds or hazard of separation of the relevant officer group versus an equivalent group that did not have any deployment. Hence, the first bar is always equal to 1.0 because it is a comparison of the nondeployers to themselves. When reading the graphs, note that bars smaller than 1.0 signify that a particular group had smaller odds or hazard of separation. Such a result is equivalent to saying that the group has a smaller probability of separation. Hence, a bar below 1.0 means that the relevant group separates at a lower rate than an equivalent group of nondeployers, and a bar greater than 1.0 indicates that the group has a higher separation rate than the equivalent group of nondeployers.

Air Force Officers

For Air Force officers, as shown in Figure 4.1, a strongly decreasing likelihood of separation is associated with an increasing number of nonhostile deployments, regardless of time period or rank. Yet, increasing the fraction of hostile deployments out of the total number of deployments tends to mitigate the positive association. Furthermore, the effect of increasing the fraction of hostile episodes for a given number of deployments is quite regular: For any time period for either junior or midgrade officers, more hostile deployment is associated with consistently increasing separation rates.[2]

However, any combination of deployment in terms of hostile and nonhostile is always associated with lower separation rates when compared with the equivalent group of nondeployers. Air Force patterns were very consistent between the junior officers and midgrade

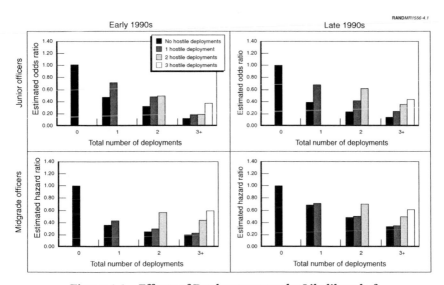

Figure 4.1—Effects of Deployment on the Likelihood of
Separation for Air Force Officers

---

[2]Note that this effect is *not* a result of model specification. The model that these results are based on was flexible enough to allow almost any pattern to emerge.

officers and temporally within each of the two groups. The result is that those who deploy remain in the service at higher rates than those who have not deployed.

Army Officers

As shown in Figure 4.2, Army officer results are similar to the Air Force officer results in that an increasing number of nonhostile deployments is associated with a decreasing rate of separation. Also, in two of the four cases (midgrade officers in the early 1990s and junior officers in the late 1990s), increasing amounts of hostile deployment tend to be associated with increasing rates of separation among officers with the same number of deployments. However, the Army results differ in two ways: (1) junior officers in the early 1990s show an increasing fraction of hostile deployments associated with *decreasing* separation rates, and (2) the hostile deployments for midgrade officers in the late 1990s have no effect.

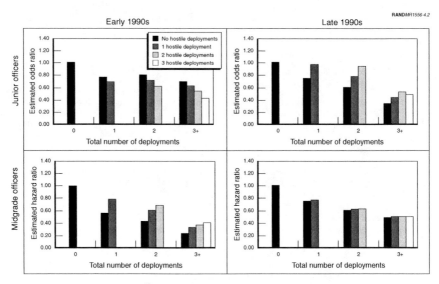

Figure 4.2—Effects of Deployment on the Likelihood of
Separation for Army Officers

Marine Corps Officers

The results for Marine Corps officers exhibit trends similar to both the Air Force and Army results. However, because there are many fewer officers in the Marine Corps compared with the other services, the final results are more variable. A clear trend shown in Figure 4.3 is that increasing episodes of nonhostile deployment are associated with decreases in the separation rate. This is consistent with the Army and Air Force results. However, increasing the fraction of hostile deployment out of the total number of episodes of deployment has a less clear-cut pattern of mitigating the rate of separation.

In one case, midgrade officers in the early 1990s who had two hostile episodes out of a total of two episodes actually experienced a greater separation rate than nondeployers (one of only two times this occurred in the analysis). Also, for midgrade officers, hostile deployment does not follow a constant trend as in the Air Force and Army: (1) in the early 1990s, those with three or more hostile deployments reversed the overall trend that an increasing fraction of

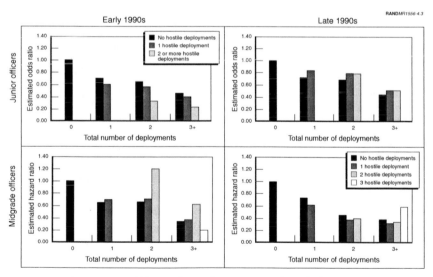

Figure 4.3—Effects of Deployment on the Likelihood of Separation for Marine Corps Officers

hostile deployment is associated with an increasing separation rate,[3] and (2) in the late 1990s, one hostile deployment was associated with a lower separation rate, when compared with those with no deployment (out of a fixed total number of deployments), but two and three or more hostile deployments are then associated with higher separation rates.

Navy Officers

As shown in Figure 4.4, with the exception of midgrade officers in the early 1990s, Navy officers with nonhostile deployment continue to follow the pattern of the other three services, though the association between increasing episodes of nonhostile deployment and decreasing separation rates are much more modest. However, unlike in the other services, junior officers with some or all hostile deployment

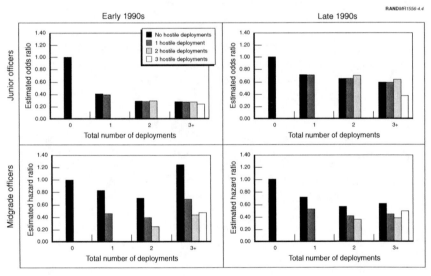

Figure 4.4—Effects of Deployment on the Likelihood of Separation for Navy Officers

---

[3]However, as mentioned, this may reflect greater sample variability because there were only a small number of instances of midgrade officers with three or more hostile deployments.

show little difference from their peers who deploy at the same rate. That is, either in the early 1990s or in the late 1990s period, the odds of separation are virtually the same regardless of the mix of hostile and nonhostile deployment.

Midgrade officers in the early 1990s show an unusual pattern in which those who have three or more nonhostile deployments have a higher rate of separation than nondeployers, in spite of the usual decreasing separation rate trend for those with one or two nonhostile deployments. In addition, unlike in the other services, within a particular number of episodes of deployment, an increasing fraction of hostile deployment is associated with a decreasing separation rate.

GENERAL JUNIOR OFFICER TRENDS

As shown in Figures 4.1–4.4, more nonhostile deployment is clearly associated with reduced odds of separation, while for a fixed number of deployments in the late 1990s, hostile deployment is at best neutral and is often associated with mitigating the positive association between deployment and retention. However, the separation rate among those who deploy, regardless of the rate of hostile deployment, is always lower than it is for those who did not deploy. For the late 1990s these results are consistent across all services.

In the early 1990s, for all services except the Air Force, the hostile deployment association is reversed, with increasing amounts of hostile deployment within a particular number of deployment episodes associated with lower odds of separation when compared with the odds for cohorts with an equivalent number of deployment episodes. A possible explanation for this reversal is that the early 1990s was a period of significant contraction in the officer corps. In fact, as was shown in Figure 2.6, between 1990 and 1996, the officer corps shrank by 22 percent. In such an environment it is possible that hostile deployments became an important way to distinguish oneself from one's peers to improve chances of either promotion or perhaps just retention. Another possible explanation is that some or all of the hostile deployment during the early 1990s (such as Operations Desert Shield and Desert Storm), when compared with the hostile deployments of the late 1990s, were inherently more rewarding so as to positively affect the career decisions of junior officers. It could also be a combination of these two factors, or one or more of these factors combined with a third. It is not possible to determine this using the existing data.

These relationships also generally hold when the deployment measure is changed from number of episodes to length to time deployed. For example, Table 4.1 shows the odds of retention for junior officers in the late 1990s period by service for various combinations of months of hostile and nonhostile deployment.[4] The major difference is that, except for the Air Force, the effect of an increasing amount of hostile deployment within a fixed total amount of deployment reverses.

GENERAL MIDGRADE OFFICER TRENDS

As with the junior officers, in the late 1990s, increasing episodes of nonhostile deployment are associated with decreasing separation rates for midgrade officers. However, except for the Air Force, the negative effect of hostile deployment tends to be mitigated for

Table 4.1

Estimated Odds Ratios by Service for the Odds of Separation
Using Length of Deployment Measures

Army			Navy			Marine Corps			Air Force		
TD	HD	OR	TD	HD	OR	TD	HD	OR	TD	HD	OR
0	0	1.00	0	0	1.00	0	0	1.00	0	0	1.00
6	0	0.65	5	0	0.26	5	0	0.79	3	0	0.36
6	4	0.59	5	3	0.23	5	3	0.57	3	3	0.54
8	0	0.64	9	0	0.23	8	0	0.77	5	0	0.29
8	4	0.58	9	3	0.21	8	3	0.55	5	3	0.45
8	7	0.53	9	5	0.18	8	4	0.50	5	4	0.47
10	0	0.62	11	0	0.23	10	0	0.70	8	0	0.23
10	4	0.56	11	3	0.21	10	3	0.50	8	3	0.35
10	7	0.52	11	5	0.18	10	4	0.46	8	4	0.37
10	9	0.48	11	6	0.17	10	5	0.43	8	7	0.43

NOTE: TD = total months of deployment; HD = months of hostile deployment; OR = odds ratio.

---

[4]The months of hostile and nonhostile deployment are based on typical lengths of deployment for each service. They were calculated as the average months of deployment for a junior officer with one, two, or three or more episodes of deployment.

midgrade officers as compared with junior officers. This difference should be expected, given that midgrade officers are self-selecting, having chosen to remain in the service after their initial service obligation. As a result, these officers have expressed an intention to make a career of the military and hence hostile deployments are less likely to have a negative association with retention. In fact, except for the Air Force, additional hostile deployment tends to be neutral and perhaps is associated with a *decreased* risk of separation.

In the early 1990s, though, increasing amounts of hostile deployment for midgrade officers in all services except the Navy were associated with increasing separation rates (among those with the same number of deployment episodes). It is possible that this too may be a result of the officer corps downsizing of that period, something that affected junior officers of all services, but one that may have manifested itself with an opposite effect. For example, one might hypothesize that, during this period of intense competition for a shrinking number of positions, hostile deployments tended to somehow interfere with promotion potential or career progression. It is also possible that midgrade officers, perhaps having decided to make a career based on their experiences in a Cold War–based military, found adding hostile deployment to decreasing career opportunities too much to bear.

These relationships generally hold when the deployment measure is changed from number of episodes to length to time deployed. Table 4.2 shows the hazard ratios for midgrade officers (for all of the 1990s) by service for various combinations of months of hostile and non-hostile deployment.[5] For midgrade officers, the results for all services except the Air Force are very similar to their late-1990s episodes results. For the Air Force, the effect of an increasing amount of hostile deployment within a fixed total amount of deployment reverses.

---

[5]As with the junior officers, the months of hostile and nonhostile deployment are based on typical lengths of deployment for each service. They were calculated as the average months of deployment for a junior officer with one, two, or three or more episodes of deployment.

Table 4.2

**Estimated Hazard Ratios by Service for the Risk of Separation
Using Length of Deployment Measures**

Army			Navy			Marine Corps			Air Force		
TD	HD	HR	TD	HD	HR	TD	HD	HR	TD	HD	HR
0	0	1.00	0	0	1.00	0	0	1.00	0	0	1.00
5	0	0.78	4	0	0.86	4	0	0.74	2	0	0.75
5	4	0.72	4	3	0.62	4	3	0.63	2	1	0.58
6	0	0.76	7	0	0.75	8	0	0.61	3	0	0.69
6	4	0.71	7	3	0.54	8	3	0.52	3	1	0.53
6	5	0.73	7	5	0.51	8	5	0.56	3	2	0.56
7	0	0.75	10	0	0.68	9	0	0.59	4	0	0.65
7	4	0.70	10	3	0.49	9	3	0.51	4	1	0.50
7	5	0.72	10	5	0.46	9	5	0.54	4	2	0.52
7	6	0.74	10	6	0.45	9	6	0.54	4	3	0.54

NOTE: TD = total months of deployment; HD = months of hostile deployment; HR = hazard ratio.

DEPLOYMENT EFFECTS BY OCCUPATION

Concerned that one or more occupational groups might be "driving" the overall model results, we also fit separate models for each occupational category within each service. While these were initially used as a check of the robustness of our overall conclusions, we were also sensitive to the possibility that results for some of the smaller occupational categories might be masked by the larger groups. Our general finding is that most occupations reflect the general trends for each service, yet there are some differences.

Tables 4.3–4.6 present the results of fitting separate models for each occupational category. However, to reduce the results to a manageable size, rather than fit six categorical indicators for low-, medium-, and high-hostile and nonhostile deployment, only two deployment variables, one for the number of hostile and another for the number of nonhostile deployment episodes, were included in the models. Such a model thus assumes a specific type of relationship between the odds of one deployment and the odds of multiple deployments,

Table 4.3

Odds Ratios for One Episode of Nonhostile Deployment by Service (for Junior Officers with Service Obligations Ending in 1997 or Later)

	Army	Navy	Marine Corps	Air Force
Acquisition	0.339	—	—	0.528
Pilot	0.612	0.208	0.460	0.664
Aviation, other	0.813	0.716	0.849	0.444
Intelligence	0.883	0.730	0.855	0.267
IT/MIS	0.899	0.899	0.454	0.475
Legal	—	0.431	0.592	0.274
Line	0.733	0.764	0.805	—
Medical	0.776	0.974	—	0.637
Nuclear	—	1.141	—	—
Personnel/ administration	1.196	0.648	0.718	0.547
Scientific/engineering	0.843	0.421	0.885	0.556
Supply	0.857	0.815	1.341	0.124

NOTE: To calculate the odds ratio for two nonhostile deployments, square the relevant odds ratio for one nonhostile deployment; to calculate the odds ratio for three nonhostile deployments, cube the relevant odds ratio for one nonhostile deployment, etc.

but that relationship is very similar to what was observed using the more flexible model with six categorical indicators.[6]

However, note that these occupational models should be interpreted with some caution because the occupational groups are quite broad. They were so defined to account for major occupational differences in retention prior to estimating the effects of deployment in the models while also allowing for comparison across the services. Nonetheless, constructing individual occupational models is instructive to determine whether particular occupations are similar or dissimilar to the entire officer corps, if for no other reason than to identify occupational fields worthy of further research and more-detailed modeling. In addition, it also allows evaluation of the

---

[6]Specifically, the odds ratio for two episodes of nonhostile deployment is equal to the odds ratio for one episode of nonhostile deployment squared; the odds ratio for three nonhostile deployments is equal to the odds ratio for one nonhostile deployment cubed, etc. A similar, but slightly more complicated, relationship holds for combinations of hostile and nonhostile deployment.

Table 4.4

Odds Ratios for One Episode of Hostile Deployment by Service (for Junior Officers with Service Obligations Ending in 1997 or Later)

	Army	Navy	Marine Corps	Air Force
Acquisition	0.320	—	—	0.891
Pilot	0.420	0.073	0.296	0.665
Aviation, other	0.840	0.426	1.085	1.162
Intelligence	0.739	1.118	1.127	0.984
IT/MIS	0.882	0.956	0.390	0.744
Legal	—	1.050	0.314	0.632
Line	0.706	0.835	0.558	—
Medical	0.726	0.799	—	0.577
Nuclear	—	1.036	—	—
Personnel/ administration	0.885	0.921	0.552	0.549
Scientific/engineering	0.549	0.380	0.750	0.879
Supply	0.782	0.788	1.157	0.595

NOTE: To calculate the desired odds ratio for an officer with X nonhostile deployments and Y hostile deployments (Y less than or equal to X) in a particular occupation, multiply the relevant odds ratio in Table 4.3 raised to the X-Y power times the contribution to the odds ratio in Table 4.4 raised to the Y power. For example, the odds ratio for an Army junior officer in an acquisition occupation who has had two hostile deployments out of three total deployments would be 0.339 × 0.320 × 0.320.

consistency of the deployment effects across the various occupational groupings.

It is important to remember that in this section, separate models were constructed for each occupational category within each service. Hence, the odds and hazard ratios are relative to the nondeployers *within that occupational category* for a particular service. In Tables 4.3–4.6, two equal odds or hazard ratios does *not* mean that the separation rates for the two occupations are equal. Rather, it means that the ratio of the odds for a given number of deployments to the odds for the nondeployers within each occupation is equal.[7]

---

[7] For example, in occupation "A" one of every two nondeploying junior officers separates, which translates into a 50-percent chance of separation for a random observation, or odds of one to one. In comparison, in occupation "A," one of every three junior officers with one nonhostile deployment separates, for a 33-percent chance, odds of one to two, and an odds ratio between the two groups of one to two divided by one to one, or one-half.

Table 4.5

Hazard Ratios of One Episode of Nonhostile Deployment by Service

	Army	Navy	Marine Corps	Air Force
Acquisition	0.790	0.766	—	0.672
Pilot	0.782	0.656	0.703	0.741
Aviation, other	0.689	0.765	0.967	0.682
Intelligence	0.692	0.838	0.800	0.521
IT/MIS	0.783	0.755	0.377	0.558
Legal	—	0.464	0.802	0.532
Line	0.800	1.134	0.791	—
Medical	0.760	0.870	—	0.685
Nuclear	—	0.777	—	—
Personnel/ administration	0.700	0.697	0.775	0.526
Scientific/engineering	0.741	0.786	1.084	0.813
Supply	0.715	0.703	0.931	0.693

NOTE: To calculate the hazard ratio for two nonhostile deployments, square the relevant hazard ratio for one nonhostile deployment; to calculate the hazard ratio for three nonhostile deployments, cube the relevant hazard ratio for one nonhostile deployment, etc.

While this may seem complicated, it actually provides the relevant comparison between the occupational groupings. That is, because various occupations are known to have significant differences in retention, the correct evaluation is how retention changes as a function of deployment relative to a baseline rate—in this case, the rate of nondeployers within that occupation.

Results

Subject to these caveats, Tables 4.3 and 4.4 show that for junior officers there are relatively few differences in deployment effects by occupational category, both between occupations within any par-

---

In occupation "B," one out of three nondeploying junior officers separates for odds of one to two. However, in occupation "B," one of every five junior officers with one nonhostile deployment separates for odds of one to four, and an odds ratio between the two groups of one-half. Thus, junior officers in occupation "B" separate at a lower rate, but for the two groups the odds of separation of the deployers relative to the odds of separation to the nondeployers are the same.

Table 4.6

Hazard Ratios of One Episode of Nonhostile Deployment by Service

	Army	Navy	Marine Corps	Air Force
Acquisition	0.474	0.632	—	0.534
Pilot	0.832	0.654	0.688	0.966
Aviation, other	0.973	0.772	0.980	0.937
Intelligence	0.808	0.629	0.971	0.869
IT/MIS	0.917	0.473	1.075	0.843
Legal	—	0.619	0.918	0.563
Line	0.877	0.788	0.759	—
Medical	0.843	0.833	—	0.824
Nuclear	—	0.580	—	—
Personnel/ administration	0.583	0.603	0.881	0.785
Scientific/engineering	0.782	0.496	1.859	0.836
Supply	0.772	0.742	0.843	0.808

NOTE: To calculate the desired hazard ratio for an officer with X nonhostile deployments and Y hostile deployments (Y less than or equal to X) in a particular occupation, multiply the relevant hazard ratio in Table 4.5 raised to the X-Y power times the relevant contribution to the hazard ratio in Table 4.6 raised to the Y power. For example, the hazard ratio for an Army midgrade officer in an acquisition occupation who has had two hostile deployments out of three total deployments would be 0.790 × 0.474 × 0.474.

ticular service and between services for any particular occupational category. Virtually all of these models—Tables 4.3 and 4.4 show the effects for 40 different models, one for each service-occupation combination listed—show that deployers have lower or very close to neutral odds of separation than do nondeployers.[8] Similarly, almost all odds for hostile deployers are lower than or basically neutral to the odds of separation for nonhostile deployers.

These results are consistent with the general service models of the previous subsection. There are particular occupations that exhibit stronger deployment effects than most of the other occupations,[9] but

---

[8]All of the odds ratios in Table 4.3 except two are less than one and the two odds ratios that are more than one are statistically insignificant.

[9]For example, most of the nonhostile deployment odds ratio estimates for the various occupations in the Army are between 0.7 and 0.9 (see the first column in Table 4.3). They are remarkably consistent across occupations and close to the estimate for the general Army model as shown in Table 4.1. However, the odds ratio estimate for the

with the exception of the legal occupation in the Navy, none significantly contradicts the general trends. This result indicates that the deployment results observed in the combined models of the previous subsections were *not driven by one occupational category* and it gives us confidence that previous results are generally applicable.

Interestingly, there are no occupational categories that show consistently low or high odds ratios across all services. There are within each service, however, sufficiently different junior officer occupations that could be further investigated and include both those with odds ratios greater than one and those with very small odds ratios. For example, acquisition occupations in the Army, pilots in the Navy and Marine Corps, and supply occupations in the Air Force all show consistently low-hostile and nonhostile odds ratios compared with other occupations within each service. Similarly, personnel/administrative occupations in the Army; nuclear and intelligence occupations in the Navy; and supply, other aviation, and intelligence occupations in the Marine Corps all show consistently high-hostile and nonhostile odds ratios compared with other occupations within each service.

Midgrade officer results are even more consistent. The hazard ratios in Tables 4.5 and 4.6 are consistent with the general model results in Table 4.2 and Figures 4.1–4.4. In particular, Table 4.6 shows that, for all services and occupations except scientific/engineering in the Marine Corps, most of the hazard ratios for episodes of hostile deployment are modest and relatively close to one.

Similar to the junior officer results, for midgrade officers there are no occupational categories that show consistent differences across all services. Midgrade officer occupations sufficiently different within each service that could be further investigated include line officers in the Navy and scientific/engineering occupations in the Marine Corps.

---

acquisition occupation is much smaller, which means that the odds of separation for nonhostile deployers in this occupation were much smaller compared with those of the nondeployers in this occupation.

Chapter Five

DISCUSSION AND CONCLUSIONS

Our findings both confirm and contradict some of the common assumptions about the association between deployment and retention of officers in the U.S. military. For example, we find a clear positive association between increasing amounts of nonhostile deployment and junior and midgrade officer retention: Officers who participate in more nonhostile deployments are retained at a higher rate in all services. Hostile deployment generally mitigates this positive effect but, in almost all cases examined, even those with some or all hostile deployment show higher retention rates than do nondeployers.

The major differences we found by service include the Air Force showing the most pronounced effect of hostile deployment and the Marine Corps and Navy showing the least effect of hostile deployment. In all services except the Air Force, in the late 1990s, we saw the effect of hostile deployment was less for midgrade officers than for junior officers.

Thus, in contradiction to the common consensus, deployment is *not* associated with higher separation. However, if we confine our attention to a specific amount of deployment in the late 1990s, higher amounts of hostile deployment are generally associated with lower retention rates compared with the rates of junior officers who have the *same* amount of nonhostile deployment. This effect is most pronounced in the Air Force, but is also true for the Army and Marine Corps. The Navy shows little effect on junior officers and a slight positive effect on midgrade officers. In fact, three of the four services show a mitigation or mild reversal of the effect of hostile deployment between junior and midgrade officers—an effect likely due to self-selection.

While we found some differences in the early 1990s, defined for the purposes of this analysis to span from 1990 through 1995, the overall, general nonhostile results were consistent with late-1990s results. One noticeable difference between the two periods was that Army and Marine Corps junior officers and Navy midgrade officers showed increased retention with increasing amounts of hostile deployment, while Marine Corps midgrade officers showed the opposite result. We hypothesize that these patterns were unique to that period, which was a time of significant contraction for the U.S. military and its officer corps. For example, from 1990 to 1996 the officer corps experienced a 22-percent reduction in size and in the early 1990s the officer corps contracted dramatically for three years in a row, shrinking 5.9 percent from 1991 to 1992, another 6.2 percent in 1993, and a further 4.4 percent in 1994.

In summary, for the time period we examined and the observed level of deployment, the fundamental pattern for junior and midgrade officers is that more deployment is associated with higher retention.[1] For junior officers, hostile deployment tends to mitigate the positive association with retention, while (except for the Air Force) for midgrade officers, it tends to have a mitigating effect in general and perhaps a slightly positive effect for midgrade Navy and Marine Corps officers.

There are a number of possible explanations for why these results are at odds with the common wisdom that deployment is bad for retention:

- **Perception versus reality.** It may be that deployment is perceived as negative when in fact it has exactly the opposite effect. For example, it could be that servicemembers find deployment to be a convenient or socially acceptable scapegoat on surveys. The evidence for long and/or hostile deployments from this work and Hosek and Totten (1998) certainly does not support the popular negative perception of deployment.

---

[1]While the discussion presented here has been in terms of episodes of deployment, additional analyses based on length of deployment provide similar results.

- **Alternate types of deployment *are* negative.** However, it also may be that the types of deployment captured with our measures have an aggregate positive effect because of their nature (as we described above), while other types of deployment we could not capture with our pay-based measures are negative. For example, it may be that short, unplanned or unforeseen deployments—not included in our data—have a strongly negative effect.[2]

- **Self-selection mechanisms.** It also could be that those officers with the greatest dislike of deployment self-select into nondeploying positions prior to exiting the military.

- **Aggregation effects.** These results characterize how aggregates of officers responded to particular patterns of hostile and non-hostile deployment. As such, they shed little light on how a particular *individual* officer would respond if he or she experienced one or more additional deployments.

ASSOCIATION VERSUS CAUSATION

Because of the third point above, we have carefully avoided any discussion about whether changes in deployment *cause* differences in officer retention. It is reasonable to expect that this is true, but given the nature of our data and an observational, retrospective study format, we cannot account for the effects of individual self-selection. Self-selection occurs because officers have at least some control over their future positions in the military. Such control implies that the officers have some influence over how likely they are to deploy because different positions have known, higher likelihoods of deploying than do others. This further implies that the associations between retention and deployment we have observed could have resulted in some significant way from each individual's choice.

For example, the observed increased retention between junior officers with no deployment and those junior officers with some deployment could be attributed to the fact that deployment is a pos-

---

[2]Some of the services have implemented efforts to make deployment more predictable, such as the Air Force reconfiguration into expeditionary forces. If the hypothesis is that unplanned and unforeseen deployment has the greatest negative effect, then efforts to improve deployment predictability should be very beneficial.

itive experience that motivates junior officers to remain in the military. However, if deployment is perceived as beneficial to selection for promotion and other advancement opportunities, then it could just as well result from career-motivated junior officers selecting billets that are more likely to deploy. These same officers, who are more likely to remain in the military, would then also be more likely to deploy.[3]

Even if deployment does not offer an advancement advantage, it is possible that those individuals who prefer military life, and are thus more likely to stay in the military, also prefer positions that are more likely to deploy. It is also possible that those left behind from deploying units are forced to work harder than their deploying counterparts, so that deployment may be causing increased attrition among those who did not deploy, not increased retention among the deployers.

With our data, we have no way of discerning whether one of these possibilities, some combination of them, or some other factor has caused the results we have observed.

HYPOTHESES UNLIKELY TO BE TRUE

While we cannot prove that more deployment causes higher retention in this study, we can cast doubt on other hypotheses.

"More Deployment Causes Lower Retention"

Our results show that more deployment—at least long and/or hostile deployment as modeled here—is associated with higher retention. If more long and/or hostile deployment caused lower retention, we would expect to see this in our data. Because we observe exactly the opposite, we can conclude that this hypothesis is not likely to be true, at least in the aggregate for populations similar to those we observed.

However, this does not mean that, on an individual-by-individual basis, more deployment might cause particular officers to have lower

---

[3]The mitigation of hostile deployment effects between junior and midgrade officers is evidence of one type of self-selection.

probabilities of remaining in the military. Nor does it mean that increased amounts of deployment, greater than what we have observed in our data, would not cause a decrease in retention.

"Hostile Deployment Is Causing Lower Retention"

For Army, Navy, and Marine Corps midgrade officers, using the same logic as in the previous case, we can conclude that this hypothesis is probably false. If this hypothesis were true, we would see greater and more-consistent effects than the data show for midgrade officers. For junior officers, on the other hand, this hypothesis may be true in the sense that among those junior officers with the same amount of deployment, we generally observe lower retention among those with a larger fraction of hostile deployment. However, hostile deployment does not result in retention rates worse than those experienced by those who do not deploy.

DIRECTIONS FOR FUTURE RESEARCH

There are a number of important directions in which to take this research. To continue the previous discussion, additional data would allow us to more carefully investigate the causal connection between deployment and officer retention. To advance such an evaluation, additional data on officer career paths would be required, and we would have to create much more detailed models. With such data and models, we could attempt to compare and contrast the retention behavior of officers with similar characteristics and career paths. Any such study would still be subject to observational study criticisms, but the more carefully we could construct homogeneous groups, the closer we could come to unraveling causes and effects.

Evaluating the Extent of Self-Selection

To put these results in proper context, it is necessary to better understand how much influence officers have on their future job assignments, and particularly how that selection impacts their likelihood of deployment *and* their likelihood of remaining on active duty. As we have previously described, it is possible that officers planning to leave active duty self-select into jobs that do not deploy prior to exiting the service. If so, then the observed association is a result of self-selection and it would be incorrect to infer that deployment causes improved retention.

Such an evaluation will be service-specific and probably occupation-specific. That is, the policies and practices that affect how much control an officer has over his or her career certainly varies by service and may also vary by occupation. An initial evaluation might entail the identification of a small number of occupations in one service and a list of unit identification codes (UICs) that deploy. From this information, we could look to see if there are significant differences in retention among those in deployable UICs and those in non-deployable UICs. For example, we could look at all surface line officers in the Navy and separate them into those assigned to ships and those who are not. If it turns out that those not assigned to ships also leave the Navy at a higher rate, then it is possible that self-selection is a factor behind some or all of the observed association. This could then be corroborated with exit interviews of particular servicemembers.

Evaluating the Effect of Short and/or Unplanned Deployments

Based on the results of this work, we hypothesize that short and/or unplanned deployments may have a negative impact on retention. That is, one explanation for the positive association we find between deployment and retention is that the impact of deployment is minimized or perhaps even completely eliminated when deployments are known in advance and the servicemember can plan for them. Also, when the deployments are of national and military significance, as is likely with those to hostile areas, then servicemembers may more readily accept a negative impact on their personal lives. If this is correct, then it also may be true that short and/or unforeseen deployments have significant negative impacts on retention. Using the same logic, it could be that because these types of deployment are hard or impossible to plan for, and perhaps because they also are of a more routine nature, servicemembers are less able to justify the deployment's negative impact.

While the deployment measures derived from pay data cannot capture short deployments, data currently being collected by DMDC and detailed service-specific data do capture this information. DMDC's data will take some time to compile given that the effort was only recently begun. In the interim, while DMDC collects enough longitudinal data to support an analysis such as the one reported on here, some work could proceed using service-specific data. For example, it may be possible to use service-specific data to derive a set of deployments, remove those already accounted for in the DMDC Perstempo dataset, and then evaluate the effect of those—the short deployments—that remain.

Accounting for Officer Quality

The military officer manning is designed around an "up or out" promotion system: To remain in the service, an officer must progress up the rank structure according to schedule or be forced to leave the service. Furthermore, because the officer corps is also strongly pyramidal, with fewer and fewer officers as rank increases, each service brings in a large quantity of junior officers and slowly sheds them over time, through either voluntary or involuntary attrition.

We have found that increasing deployments are associated with higher retention rates. However, what would presumably be of more interest to the military is determining whether deployment affects the retention of high-quality officers. Unfortunately, there is no measure of officer quality in the current dataset, so we currently cannot tell if deployments have a differential effect by quality.

Future work could seek to derive a measure of officer quality and then test the effect of deployments on the high-quality officers. There are no readily available measures of quality, and for junior officers there is virtually no variation in the obvious surrogate measures, such as time in grade. Development of such quality measures will not be trivial because the data are not likely to be readily available, nor will they be easily amenable to simple algorithmic derivations. However, there are some communities within the officer corps that might lend themselves to simpler measures of quality. For example, in the medical community, specific medical qualifications and certifications could be used to measure quality. These are obviously related to medical officer quality and should be readily available.

Detailed Modeling of Specific Communities

Whether or not quality is incorporated into the models, more-detailed models of specific officer communities would provide more information. The current models account for community differences only in the broadest manner. For example, all pilots are assigned to one occupational category even though there are certainly differences in deployment by aircraft type. Detailed modeling would allow us to better account for differences within each community and to more carefully investigate the causal question. For example, hostile deployment seems to have a very negative effect for Navy junior officers in legal occupations. This is very different from all other Navy occupational categories.

MODELING METHODOLOGY

Standard statistical models were used for both the junior officer and midgrade officer models. In an interesting deviation from the usual employment of these models, however, we hold virtually the entire population of (eligible) military officers in our data. Thus, we are not using the models for making inference to a larger population from a sample; rather, we are using the models to parsimoniously summarize the relationship between retention and deployment, after accounting for other factors that affect retention.

JUNIOR OFFICER METHODOLOGY

The model for junior officer retention after completion of initial service obligation is based on logistic regression techniques. Logistic regression is a standard statistical technique for modeling data with binary outcomes, such as whether or not an officer remained on active duty after his or her initial service obligation. Detailed discussions and the mathematical development of the technique can be found in such textbooks as McCullaugh and Nelder (1991) or Hosmer and Lemeshow (1989). The basic form of the model is

$$\log\left(\frac{p}{1-p}\right) = \beta_0 + \beta_1 X_1 + \cdots + \beta_n X_n + \varepsilon,$$

where p is the probability that an officer will separate within one year after the expiration of his or her initial service obligation. The ratio of $p/(1-p)$ is referred to as the odds. The β coefficients in the model represent the change in the log odds for a unit change in an X

covariate. The Xs capture the various demographic differences in the population, such as gender, race, occupation, and rate of deployment. In logistic regression, the log odds are assumed to be a linear function of various covariates.

The odds are defined as the probability that an officer with a particular set of characteristics will separate from the military divided by the probability that he or she will not. The odds can be any number between zero and infinity. Odds of one mean that an officer with those characteristics is equally likely to separate as not. Odds of less than one mean that such an officer is less likely to separate, and odds greater than one mean the officer is more likely to separate.

Through algebraic manipulation, we can explicitly estimate the probability of retention, $\hat{p}$ as a function of the coefficients:

$$\hat{p} = \frac{\exp\left(\hat{\beta}_0 + \hat{\beta}_1 X_1 + \cdots + \hat{\beta}_n X_n\right)}{1 + \exp\left(\hat{\beta}_0 + \hat{\beta}_1 X_1 + \cdots + \hat{\beta}_n X_n\right)},$$

where the $\hat{\beta}$s are the coefficients estimated from the data via maximum likelihood.

Unfortunately, changes in $\hat{p}$ are not linear with changes in the $\hat{\beta}$s, so there is no simple way to summarize how the $\hat{\beta}$s directly affect the probability of retention over all possible ranges. However, $\exp(\hat{\beta}_i)$ can be interpreted as the odds ratio (OR) when X_i is a binary characteristic. The odds ratio is simply the ratio of the odds when $X_i = 1$ versus $X_i = 0$. The odds ratio is roughly equivalent to the relative risk.[1] If $OR = 2$, then we interpret this to mean that officers with characteristic $X_i = 1$ are twice as likely to separate from the service as those with $X_i = 0$.

For the occupation-specific models in Tables 4.3 and 4.4, when X_i is the number of nonhostile deployments and X_j is the number of

---

[1] When probability of an event is rare, then the odds ratio is very close to the relative risk. When the odds ratio is greater than one and the probability of the event is not rare, then the odds ratio overstates the relative risk. Conversely, when the odds ratio is less than one and the probability of the event is not rare, then the odds ratio understates the relative risk.

hostile deployments $X_j \leq X_i$, $[\exp(\hat{\beta}_i)]^{X_i}[\exp(\hat{\beta}_j)]^{X_j}$ is the odds ratio for officers having the specified type and number of deployments versus those with no deployment. The values listed in Tables 4.3 and 4.4 are the exponentiated model coefficients.

MIDGRADE OFFICER METHODOLOGY

The models for midgrade officer retention are based on survival-analysis techniques. Survival analysis is a standard statistical technique for modeling the time to an event. In this case, we model the time until separation from the service using Cox nonproportional hazard models. We employ this modeling methodology for midgrade officers because it accounts for both the occurrence and the timing of separation. Other methods, such as logistic regression used for junior officers, ignore information about timing. In the case of junior officers, this was appropriate. For midgrade officers who can leave at any time, timing is important information. We use the Cox model to allow for time-varying covariates. For example, over time an officer may get married, be promoted, acquire advanced education, etc., and these changes in life status may affect his or her decision to stay in or leave the military.

Another major advantage of survival-analysis methodology is that it is designed to account for "censoring," which occurs when the data ends before the event of interest is observed. For example, the Perstempo data end in September 1999; at that point many officers in the database were still on active duty. We know when each officer was commissioned, and all information about each through September 1999, but for those still on active duty in September 1999 we do not know if or when they left the service. Censoring is not easily handled with methods like logistic regression, but it is perfectly straightforward in survival analysis. Detailed discussions and the mathematical development of the technique can be found in Hosmer and Lemeshow (1999). Information on SAS implementation can be found in Allison (1995).

In survival analysis, the time until an event occurs (separation) is modeled as a realization of a random process. To describe the probability distribution of event times, the hazard function is used. The hazard function, in essence, is defined as the probability of the event occurring in period $t + 1$, given that it did not occur in period t. Formally, the hazard function, $h(t)$, is defined as

$$h(t) = \lim_{\Delta t \to 0} \frac{P\{t \leq T < \Delta t \mid T \geq t\}}{\Delta t}.$$

Thus, the hazard function is the instantaneous probability that an event will occur at exactly time t, given that it has not occurred previously. For this work, it is the probability that an individual leaves the service (T) at time t, given that he or she was on active duty at time t.

For person i, the Cox nonproportional model expresses the hazard as

$$h_i(t) = h_0(t) \exp\left\{\beta_1 X_{i1}(t) + \cdots + \beta_k X_{ik}(t)\right\},$$

where $h_0(t)$ is an unspecified *baseline hazard function*, the β coefficients are solved using partial maximum likelihood, and the Xs are the data. The ts in parentheses indicate that the data (for example, rank) may vary with time. However, others, such as gender or race, may be constant.

The Cox model is a semiparametric model because the baseline hazard function is not specified. Rather, the model output is the hazard ratio (HR) defined as

$$HR(t) = \frac{h_0(t) \exp\left\{\hat{\beta}_1 X_{i1}(t) + \cdots + \hat{\beta}_k X_{ik}(t)\right\}}{h_0(t) \exp\left\{\hat{\beta}_1 X_{j1}(t) + \cdots + \hat{\beta}_k X_{jk}(t)\right\}}.$$

For two subjects with similar characteristics except $X_{ik}(t) = 1$ and $X_{jk}(t) = 0$, then $HR(t) = \exp\{\hat{\beta}_k\}$. Note that $h_0(t)$ simply cancels in the ratio. Also note that this model is a generalization of the well-known Cox proportional hazard model. The nonproportional model here results because the data are allowed to depend on time.

One appealing aspect of this model is the ability to interpret *HR* as a relative risk-type ratio.[2]   That is, in the case illustrated above, if $HR(t) = 2$ then we interpret this to mean that officers with character-istic $X_{ik}(t) = 1$ are twice as likely to leave the service at time t as those with $X_{jk}(t) = 0$.

For the occupation-specific models in Tables 4.5 and 4.6, when X_i is the number of nonhostile deployments and X_j is the number of hos-tile deployments $X_j \leq X_i$, $[\exp(\hat{\beta}_i)]^{X_i}[\exp(\hat{\beta}_j)]^{X_j}$ is the hazard ratio for officers having the specified type and number of deployments versus officers with no deployment.   The values listed in Tables 4.5 and 4.6 are the exponentiated model coefficients.

---

[2]A *relative risk ratio* is a comparison of the probability of an event occurring for two groups. It is the ratio of the probability of the event occurring for one individual with a particular trait versus the probability of the same event occurring for a similar individual without the trait. In this case, it is the probability of separation (the hazard) for an individual with a certain level and type of deployment to a similar individual without any deployment. If the ratio is larger than one, there is a higher risk of separation for those who deploy than for those who do not; if it is less than one, then the risk is less for those who deploy.

DETAILED REGRESSION RESULTS

JUNIOR OFFICERS

Table B.1 provides the model parameter estimates for each service's main junior officer models. Note that, as in the body of the report, these models estimate the probability of separation. The underlying statistical methodology was previously described in Appendix A.

The baseline group consists of single, white, male, non-academy line officers (pilots in the Air Force) with no deployment and with a minimum service obligation that expired in 1998. The odds ratios in the body of this report, then, compare an equivalent officer with one demographic changed to this baseline group.

Table B.1

Logistics Regression Model Parameter Estimates for Each Service

	Army	Navy	Marine Corps	Air Force
Intercept	−0.3560*	0.3274*	−0.4118*	−2.6387*
Indicator for Number of Deployments				
One	−0.2686*	−0.8883*	−0.3657*	−0.7681*
Two	−0.2266*	−1.2206*	−0.4406*	−1.1799*
Three or more	−0.3643*	−1.2521*	−0.7931*	−2.1787*
Indicator for Number of Hostile Deployments				
One	−0.1119	−0.0306	−0.1489	0.4119*

Table B.1—continued

	Army	Navy	Marine Corps	Air Force
Two	−0.2530	−0.0061	—	0.4437
Three or more	−0.4972	−0.1492	−0.7176	1.1484*
Indicator for Number of Deployments and "Window" After 1995				
One	−0.0296	0.5506*	0.0457	−0.2055
Two	−0.2895*	0.7927*	0.0595	−0.2875
Three or more	−0.7278*	0.7237*	−0.0355	0.1335
Indicator for Number of Hostile Deployments and "Window" After 1995				
One	0.3701*	0.0271	0.2971	0.1633
Two	0.6981*	0.0834	—	0.5304
Three or more	0.8664*	−0.3117	0.8586*	0.0434
Occupation				
Scientific/engineering	0.0108	−0.7970*	−0.1741	0.9295*
Intelligence	−0.2437*	−1.0174*	0.0570	0.8265*
Nuclear	—	1.3062*	—	—
Personnel/ administration	−0.3104*	−0.9376*	0.2607	0.4146*
Acquisition	−0.3977*	—	—	0.9699*
Supply	−0.0158	−0.3232*	0.6797*	1.2156*
Medical	−0.1715*	−0.4128*	—	1.3567*
Pilot	−1.2900*	−1.5958*	−2.0315*	—
Other aviation	−1.2417*	−0.2513*	0.3166*	1.3654*
IT/MIS	0.0788	−0.6204*	0.5925*	1.1437*
Legal	—	0.0795	−1.4826*	0.6752*
Student	−0.7794*	—	—	1.0924*
Religious	—	−1.4189*	—	—
Other	−0.4049*	−0.9631*	−0.6450*	1.9445*
Female	0.5585*	0.0409	−0.1571	0.5263*
Has Dependents	−0.3009*	−0.3793*	−0.3617*	−0.1129*
Academy	0.2334*	−0.0462	−0.5917*	0.0699
Race				
African American	−0.1525*	−0.1241	−0.1263	−0.2333*
Hispanic	0.0883	0.1725*	0.1306	−0.2410
Asian	−0.2048*	−0.1144	—	−0.1047
Other	0.0739	0.0698	−0.0762	0.1420
Years				
1991	−2.2757*	−1.9189*	−2.1910*	−1.6227*

Table B.1—continued

	Army	Navy	Marine Corps	Air Force
1992	−1.7906*	−2.1952*	−1.4021*	−1.5287*
1993	−0.2873*	−0.6141*	0.4956*	−0.4351*
1994	0.1082*	−0.0920	0.3734*	0.3949*
1995	0.2071*	−0.1004	0.5993*	0.6099*
1996	0.2189*	−0.1681*	0.4085*	0.7814*
1997	0.3948*	0.3408*	0.4914*	0.7851*

NOTE: * indicates statistical significance at $p < 0.05$.

MIDGRADE OFFICERS

Table B.2 provides the parameter estimates for the report's main midgrade officer models for each service. The baseline group consists of O-3 single, white, male line officers (pilots in the Air Force) with a bachelor's degree and who had no deployment in 1998.

The underlying statistical methodology was previously described in Appendix A. As discussed in Appendix A, the hazard ratios in the main body of the report can be roughly interpreted as a relative risk. This means, for example, that if the $HR = 2$, then officers with the characteristic in question are twice as likely to leave the service as those without.

Table B.2

Survival Model Parameter Estimates for Each Service

Variable	Army	Navy	Marine Corps	Air Force
Number of Deployments				
One	−0.5813*	−0.1837*	−0.4406*	−1.0341*
Two	−0.8292*	−0.3431*	−0.4416*	−1.4163*
Three or more	−1.4241*	0.2193	−1.0724*	−1.6680*
Number of Hostile Deployments				
One	0.3340*	−0.5873*	0.0825	0.1921
Two	0.4542	−1.0380*	0.6169	0.8429*
Three or more	0.5406	−0.9468*	−0.5313	1.1405*

Table B.2—continued

Variable	Army	Navy	Marine Corps	Air Force
Indicator for Number of Deployments and "Window" After 1995				
One	0.2831*	−0.1476	0.1337	0.6524*
Two	0.3126	−0.2283	−0.3621	0.6706*
Three or more	0.6815	−0.7169*	0.0940	0.5579
Indicator for Number of Hostile Deployments and "Window" After 1995				
One	−0.3134*	0.2731*	−0.2702	−0.1473
Two	−0.4200	0.5759*	−0.7497*	−0.4303
Three or more	−0.5001	0.7440	0.9503	−0.5063
Rank				
O-2	1.8759*	1.3386*	2.4044*	1.4217*
O-4	0.4387*	−0.9649*	−0.5401*	0.4228*
Promoted within last year	−0.7697*	−0.2173*	−0.1559	−1.6428*
Education				
Master's degree	0.1438*	−0.3673*	0.3256*	−0.1990*
Ph.D.	−0.3761	0.5594*	0.4880	−0.0570
Earned degree last two years	−0.6851*	−1.2758*	−0.8007*	−0.6183*
Has Dependents	−0.1593*	−0.3308*	−0.3408*	−0.1252*
Female	0.3169*	−0.2340*	0.1234	0.3498*
Race				
African American	−0.3471*	−0.2534*	−0.4178*	−0.2815*
Hispanic	−0.0686	0.0164	0.0096	−0.2405
Other	−0.0315	0.0230	−0.0602	0.0710
Occupation				
Scientific/engineering	−0.0113	0.3472*	−0.4974*	−0.2711*
Intelligence	−0.0311	−0.3945*	−0.2007	−0.6002*
Personnel/ administration	−0.2587*	0.1377*	0.0245	−0.6297*
Nuclear	—	0.2416*	—	—
Acquisition	−0.2752*	—	—	−0.5241*
Medical	−0.0113	0.0151	—	−0.4617*
Religious	—	−0.3224	—	—
Student	−1.4204*	—	—	−1.3554*
Other	−0.0420	−0.0960	—	−0.5562*
Supply	0.0662	−0.0513	0.1428	−0.7975*
Pilot	0.2288*	0.2187*	0.5761*	—

Table B.2—continued

Variable	Army	Navy	Marine Corps	Air Force
Other aviation	0.5569*	0.5517*	–0.3623*	–0.7809*
IT/MIS	0.0197	–0.0183	0.1516	0.0940
Legal	—	0.4194*	0.1763	–0.2133*
Years				
1993	–0.9310*	0.4590	–1.5548*	–0.6347*
1994	–0.4561*	0.8514*	–0.0544	–0.4792*
1995	–0.3675*	0.3820*	–0.3743*	–0.4056*
1996	–0.2299*	0.2137*	0.0135	–0.5657*
1997	–0.2287*	0.0601	0.0675	–0.3016*
1998	–0.1190*	–0.0747	–0.1937*	–0.1306*

NOTE: * indicates statistical significance at $p < 0.05$.

OFFICER RETENTION WITH RESPECT TO OTHER DEMOGRAPHICS

Demographic covariates were included in the junior and midgrade officer models to control for various factors affecting retention prior to evaluating the effect of deployment on officer separation. However, these variables can be interpreted in their own right and they provide interesting information about other factors related to retention.

Tables C.1 and C.2 provide the odds and hazard ratios for the relevant demographic factors in the junior and midgrade officer models. (Appendix B presents the complete set of parameter estimates for all of the models.)

Tables C.1 and C.2 show quite consistent effects for gender, family status, and race. Both the Army and Air Force have higher separation rates for junior and midgrade female officers compared with male officers; in the Marine Corps, they are statistically neutral. For the Navy, rates are insignificant for junior officers and, in a departure from consistency, midgrade female officers showed a *lower* separation rate.

Across all services and ranks, officers with families are more likely to remain on active duty compared with their single colleagues. Also consistent across all of the service models, the odds ratios for the junior officers are smaller than or equal to the hazard ratios for the midgrade officers, which can be interpreted to mean that junior officers with dependents are more likely to be retained past their initial service obligation date as compared with their single peers than are those midgrade officers with dependents, compared with their peers.

Table C.1

Odds Ratios for Junior Officer Model Demographics by Service

	Army	Navy	Marine Corps	Air Force
Female	1.748*	1.042	0.855	1.693*
Has Dependents	0.740*	0.684*	0.697*	0.893*
Academy	1.263*	0.955	0.553*	1.072
Race				
African American	0.859*	0.883	0.881	0.792*
Hispanic	1.092	1.188*	1.140	0.786
Asian	0.815*	0.892	—	0.901
Other	1.077	1.072	0.927	1.153

NOTE: * indicates statistical significance at p < 0.05.

Table C.2

Hazard Ratios for Midgrade Officer Model Demographics by Service

	Army	Navy	Marine Corps	Air Force
Female	1.383*	0.791*	1.131	1.419*
Has Dependents	0.853*	0.718*	0.711*	0.882*
Race				
African American	0.707*	0.776*	0.658*	0.755*
Hispanic	0.934	1.017	1.010	0.786*
Other	0.969	1.023	0.942	0.931

NOTE: * indicates statistical significance at p < 0.05.

With respect to racial differences, at the midgrade ranks minority officers are less likely to leave active duty than their white counterparts. This effect is statistically significant for the comparison between African American midgrade officers and white midgrade officers, though for the other minority categories, the hazard ratios are generally not statistically significant. Similar effects for African Americans resulted in the junior officer models, though the differences for the Navy and Marine Corps were not statistically significant. The one departure from this trend was with Hispanic Navy junior officers who are slightly more likely to leave active duty as compared with their white peers (OR = 1.2). The Army and Marine

Corps also showed hazard ratios greater than one, but they were not statistically significant.

Finally, in the junior officer models there are differing effects for those officers who graduated from their service's military academy. West Point graduates in the Army are more likely to leave active duty after their minimum service obligation as compared with their non-academy peers. In the Marine Corps the effect is the opposite; in the Navy and Air Force the effect is statistically insignificant and the estimated odds ratios are very close to one.

What is striking about Tables C.1 and C.2 is how consistent many of the effects are across the services. It is striking because the models were fit separately for each service. Such consistency lends credibility to the deployment results and the likelihood that the observed results are not an artifact of one particular service's personnel policies or practices.

DEFINITION OF OCCUPATIONAL CATEGORIES

The occupation categories for each service were defined according to the rules in the following tables (D.1–D.4) using the Service Occupation Codes for the Army, Air Force, and Marine Corps and both the Service and Duty Occupation Codes for the Navy. The code definitions were taken from the *Occupational Conversion Index* published by the Office of the Assistant Secretary of Defense for Personnel and Readiness (1997).

Table D.1

Mapping of Three-Digit Area of Concentration (AOC) Codes to Occupational Categories for the Army

Occupational Category	AOC Codes
Acquisition	5-- (except 53A, 53B, 53C, 53X, 55A, 55B, 550, 56A, 56D)
Pilot	15A, 15B, 152, 153, 154, 155
Aviation, other	15C, 15D, 150, 151
Intelligence	3--
IT/MIS	25B, 25C, 25D, 25E, 53A, 53B, 53C, 53X
Legal	55A, 55B, 550
Line	1-- (except 15A, 15B, 15C, 15D, 150, 151, 152, 153-, 154, 155)
Medical	6--, 7--
Personnel/administration	41-, 42-, 43-, 44-, 45-, 46-
Religious	56A, 56D
Scientific/engineering	2-- (except 25B, 25C, 25D, 25E), 47-, 48-, 49-

Table D.1—continued

Occupational Category	AOC Codes
Supply	8--, 9--
Student	00E
Other	All other codes except if code is missing.

NOTE: "-" indicates position may assume any alphanumeric character.

Table D.2

Mapping of Four-Digit Designator Codes and Navy Officer Billet Classification (NOBC) Codes to Occupational Categories for the Navy

Occupational Category	Designator Codes	NOBC Codes
Acquisition	—	216-, 2170, 218-, 2192, 8018, 60--, 62--, 63--, 67--
Pilot	13--, 154-	85--, 8653, 8670, 8672, 8673, 8675, 8680, 8685, 8687, 8694, 8696
Aviation, other	731-, 732-, 734-, 736-, 738-	8026, 8112, 86-- (except 8653, 8670, 8672, 8673, 8675, 8680, 8685, 8687, 8694, 8696), 89--
Intelligence	161-, 163-, 745-	96--, 98--
IT/MIS	619-, 629-, 642-, 719-, 729-, 742-	2612, 2614, 2642, 2748, 5913, 5917, 5970, 9705, 9710, 9715, 9720, 9730, 9735, 9740, 9745, 9750, 9755, 9560, 9590, 9595, 9781
Legal	25--	25--, 3415
Line	11--, 17--, 61-- (except 619-), 62-- (except 629-), 63--, 71-- (except 719-), 72-- (except 729-)	90--, 92--, 93-- (except 9371, 9372, 9373, 9374, 9392, 9393, 9394), 94--, 95-- (except 9560, 9590, 9595)
Medical	19--, 21--, 22--, 23--, 27--, 29--	0---
Nuclear	640-, 670-	7249, 7251, 7273, 7968, 9371, 9372, 9373, 9374, 9392, 9393, 9394, 9905, 9920
Personnel/ administration	641-, 741-	26-- (excluding 2612, 2614, 2642), 3020, 3035, 3120, 3125, 3126, 3127, 3320, 3330, 3350, 34-- (excluding 3415), 3910, 3925, 3943, 3950, 3965, 3970, 3981, 3985, 5761

Table D.2—continued

Occupational Category	Designator Codes	NOBC Codes
Religious	410-	35--, 37--
Scientific/engineering	14--, 15--, 51--	20--, 2105, 2145, 215-, 2175, 2176, 2190, 22--, 23--. 32--, 4---, 59-- (except 5913, 5917, 5970), 64--, 65--, 69--, 7--- (except 7249, 7251, 7273, 7968), 8002, 8004, 8015, 8050, 8074, 8076
Supply	31-- ,65--, 751-, 75-- 1---	
Other	All other codes except if both primary and duty codes are missing.	

NOTE: "-" indicates position may assume any alphanumeric character.

Table D.3

Mapping of Four-Digit Military Occupational Specialty (MOS) Codes to Occupational Categories for the Marine Corps

Occupational Category	MOS Codes
Acquisition	9956, 9957, 9958, 9959, 9962
Pilot	73--, 75-- (except 7599), 9965, 9967, 9969
Aviation, other	60--, 63--, 65--, 66--, 68--, 70--, 72--, 9966
Intelligence	02--, 26--
IT/MIS	2802, 2805, 2810, 4002, 4010, 5970, 9628, 9636, 9646, 9648, 9658, 9975, 9985
Legal	44--, 9683, 9684, 9685, 9686, 9687, 9688, 9914
Line	03--, 04--, 08--, 18--, 23--, 25--, 57--, 58--, 99-- (except 9913, 9914, 9956, 9957, 9958, 9959, 9962, 9965, 9966, 9967, 9969, 9975, 9985), XX01
Personnel/administration	01--, 34--, 43--, 46--, 55--, 9640, 9644, 9674, 9676, 9678, 9680, 98--
Scientific/engineering	11--, 13--, 9602, 9650, 9652, 9620, 9622, 9624, 9626, 9630, 9631, 9632, 9634, 9670
Supply	21--, 28-- (except 2802, 2805, 2810), 30--, 31--, 33--, 35--, 41--, 59--, 9913
Student	7599
Other	All other codes except if code is missing.

NOTE: "-" indicates position may assume any alphanumeric character.

Table D.4

Mapping of Five-Digit Air Force Specialty (AFS) Codes to Occupational Categories for the Air Force

Occupational Category	AFS Codes
Acquisition	63--- (except 63A1A, 63A3A), 64---, 65---
Pilot	11---, 12---, 80---, 81---, 91---, 97---
Aviation, other	1---- (except 11---, 14---), 33--- (except 33S1-, 33S3-, 33S1A, 33S1B, 33S1C, 33S3A, 33S3B, 33S3C)
Intelligence	14---
IT/MIS	33S1-, 33S3-, 33S1A, 33S1B, 33S1C, 33S3A, 33S3B, 33S3C, 62E1C, 62E3C, 62E1E, 62E3E, 63A1A, 63A3A
Legal	51---, 92J0-
Medical	4----
Personnel/administration	35---, 36---, 38---, 83---, 84---, 85---
Religious	52---
Scientific/engineering	6---- (except 62E1C, 62E3C, 62E1E, 62E3E, and 63---), 32---
Supply	2----
Student	92T--, 92J1-, 92J2-, 92J3-, 92M0-, 92M1-, 92M2-
Other	All other codes except if code is missing.

NOTE: "-" indicates position may assume any alphanumeric character.

Allison, P. D., *Survival Analysis Using the SAS System: A Practical Guide,* Cary, N.C.: SAS Institute, 1995.

Defense Manpower Data Center (DMDC), *1999 Survey of Active Duty Personnel,* Vol. 1, *Assignments, Careers, and Military Life,* DMDC Report No. 2000-006, September 2000.

Gordon, D. M., D. W. Gelfeld, and D. L. Smith, eds., *2001 Uniformed Services Almanac,* Falls Church, Va.: Uniformed Services Almanac, Inc., 2001.

Hosek, J., and M. Totten, *Does Perstempo Hurt Reenlistment? The Effect of Long or Hostile Perstempo on Reenlistment,* Santa Monica, Calif.: RAND, MR-990-OSD, 1998.

Hosmer, D. W., Jr., and S. Lemeshow, *Applied Logistic Regression,* New York: John Wiley & Sons, 1989.

____, *Applied Survival Analysis: Regression Modeling of Time to Event Data,* New York: John Wiley & Sons, 1999.

McCullaugh, P., and J. A. Nelder, *Generalized Linear Models,* 2nd edition, New York: Chapman and Hall, 1991.

Office of the Assistant Secretary of Defense for Personnel and Readiness, *Occupational Conversion Index: Enlisted/Officer/Civilian,* Department of Defense (DoD 1312.1-1), March 1997.

Office of the Secretary of Defense, *Military Compensation Background Papers: Compensation Elements and Related Manpower*

Cost Items, Their Purposes and Legislative Backgrounds, 5th edition, Washington, D.C.: Superintendent of Documents, U.S. Government Printing Office, September 1996.

Office of the Under Secretary of Defense for Personnel and Readiness (OUSD[P&R]), *Population Representation in the Military Services: Fiscal Year 1999,* Department of Defense, November 2000.

Peters, K. M., "The Price of Peace," *GovExec.com.* Online at www.govexec.com/features/0397s2.htm (as of April 17, 2002), March 1997.

U.S. General Accounting Office (GAO), *Military Personnel: Perspectives of Surveyed Service Members in Retention Critical Specialties,* briefing report to congressional requesters, GAO/NSAID-99-197BR, August 1999.